Strong bodies, strong business

A STEP-BY-STEP GUIDE TO BUILDING
A SUSTAINABLE BUSINESS THROUGH WEIGHTLIFTING

JANET MAJURE

BREAD BASKET PUBLISHING COMPANY

Printed in the United States of America
First Printing, 2018
ISBN 978-0-9656695-1-1

Breadbasket Publishing Company
Lawrence, Kansas
bbasketpub@gmail.com

Book designer: Amanda Warren Martin, Fort Collins, Colorado (www.amandawarren.com)
Editor: Lynn Byczynski, Lawrence, Kansas
Copy Editor: Linda Finestone, Los Angeles, California
Proofreader: Karen Johnson, Lawrence, Kansas
Cover photo (top): © 2018, Earl Richardson, Lawrence, Kansas (www.earlrichardson.com)
Cover photo (bottom): © www.123rf.com / David Kashakhi
Contents page photos (left to right): © www.123rf.com / Jozef Polc / Dean Drobot / Jozef Polc
Back cover photo (center): © www.123rf.com / Alexey Poprotsky
Back cover author photo: © 2018, Amy Lee, Lawrence, Kansas
All other photos © 2018, Janet Majure

DISCLAIMER: Every effort has been made to ensure that the information in this book was correct at time of publication. The author and publisher, however, hereby disclaim any liability to any party for any loss, damage, or disruption caused by errors or omissions, whether such errors or omissions result from negligence, accident, or any other cause. Information in this book is meant to supplement, not replace, proper weightlifting training.

TRADEMARK ACKNOWLEDGMENTS

CrossFit, Bodypump, and Certified Strength and Conditioning Specialist are trademarks or registered trademarks and the property of their respective owners, as are any other trademarks mentioned in this text.

To my daughter, for my confidence in her

To my clients, for their confidence in me

CONTENTS

INTRODUCTION

If you are a weightlifter, a personal trainer, a sports coach, or perhaps a group exercise instructor—whether for spinning, aerobic dance, yoga, or other activity—you probably should be teaching weightlifting. Really. And if you like the idea of running your clients' workouts the way you prefer and relating to your clients in a meaningful way, then you might think about starting your own business as a weightlifting coach. This book shows you how.

Teaching weightlifting to mostly middle-aged people, mostly women, is what I've been doing the last six and a half years, and clients continually reward me with comments telling about their most recent successes outside the weight room that they attribute to weightlifting. In my many years of employment, I've never done anything as satisfying. It feels great to know you are helping people in a concrete way, and it's even nicer when they tell you—and they do!

In fact, I'd go so far as to declare that by focusing on a demographic often over-looked in the fitness industry—people, especially women, older than 45—you can build a thriving and personally rewarding business, too. With that demographic, you get a clientele that makes remarkable, life-changing gains—and is grateful for it. And, unlike the highly mobile, younger demographic, they keep coming back. Don't believe me? Consider the comments my clients offered when I put up my website a few years ago:

- "I have taken weightlifting classes and used machines at a gym, but following Janet's systematic approach is the first time I have had measurable results in terms of strength. Plus, I have maintained my bone density without medication, and I feel and look better." —*Angela, age 65*

- "I realized my grandkids weren't as heavy as I thought they were months before. It became less of a big deal to put something heavy way up on the top shelf. My knees didn't kill me anymore when in one position for too long. I could squat down and play with the kids ... be the catcher for the impromptu family baseball games. My bike rides became real bike rides again. I felt like I could climb a mountain with all this newfound strength." —*Pam, age 45*

- "Since starting weightlifting 18 months ago, not only have I gotten stronger (I no longer need help carrying my dog's 40-pound bag of food to the car!), but my balance and stamina have improved." —*Linda, age 54*

- "I love my weightlifting class! I was apprehensive, because in the past I've hated those weights-aerobics classes. This is a completely different experience! I can feel my newfound strength regularly in everyday life. Plus, it's a great way to blow off steam! I recommend it to everyone I meet wanting to improve their fitness!" —*Susan, 27*

- "I always feel my workout is tailored to my abilities. I appreciate Janet's observations and advice. Instead of just not going downhill, I am getting stronger. It is also a fun group to work with." —*Michael, 67*

Comments such as these are typical of the kind of remarks I hear week in and week out. Wouldn't you like that?

I don't exclude younger people from my classes. The 20- and 30-year-olds in my classes are outnumbered, but their comments are rewarding, too, both because it's nice to hear their enthusiasm about weightlifting, and because they say they are inspired and motivated by the strength of their older classmates. Esprit de corps develops, too, and on days when workouts are particularly heavy, my clients cheer each other on.

I understand how they feel, having experienced remarkable strength gains since I started weightlifting. And I am right there with you if want a rewarding career coaching weightlifting.

MY STORY

I never expected I'd be a weightlifting coach. When I started weightlifting, it was with one goal in mind: to build my weakened bones without resorting to drugs. Little did I imagine that seven years later, I would start my own business teaching weightlifting; it wasn't an obvious career move for someone with decades of experience as a writer and editor. But teaching and coaching weight-lifting is now my primary occupation, and it's been enormously satisfying as well as financially worthwhile.

I was 51 years old when I started lifting, freshly recovered from a compression fracture of a lumbar vertebra (after an embarrassing fall off an electric scooter). Before the fracture, I was reasonably active. I walked at least two miles a day, seven days a week. I lived in a house with stairs I traversed many times a day. I did my own cleaning and gardening and snow-shoveling. I didn't go to a gym, but I tried to incorporate physical activity regularly into my everyday life.

My first day at weightlifting shocked me into the reality of just how much strength I'd lost over the years. I couldn't do a single bodyweight squat. I could maybe get to about a 45-degree knee bend without feeling unsteady. Because of the previous fracture, I was terrified of trying a Romanian deadlift, although I know it was very light. The only gratifying aspect of that first day was that the coach told me I did well on the power clean intro. A day and a half later, I was unbelievably sore. My quadriceps screamed. And that was from working out with a broomstick! And my abdominals! Oof!

Despite that horrifying start, I stuck with it. For at least the first month, I spent the entire workout dreading the core work at the end of the session. After a couple of months, I concluded that I needed to resign myself to being sore at least a couple of days a week as long as I continued to lift.

But I got stronger. (Surprise!) One day I simply stood up from a chair and realized I was stronger. Standing up doesn't sound like much, but without realizing it, I'd started to develop the habits of feeble people—such as using my hands to help me stand up from a chair or using a little rocking momentum to get out of the car. Now I didn't need those habits. That's big! A vanity reinforcement occurred about that time, too. That was the night when I turned onto my side in bed, laid my hand on my thigh, and discovered that my thigh had become nice and solid.

And all that was within the first six months or so. As I continued to lift, I continued to get stronger. (So did my bones.) As is common, I plateaued relatively early on my bench presses and bent-over rows, but for years I kept making gains in my squats, Romanian deadlifts, and power cleans. A major highlight was squatting 60 kg—for reps! my body weight!—around the time of my 60th birthday. It was a great feeling! And I've added to that in the three years since.

CHANGING ROLES

About the sixth year of my lifting, my coach, Loren McVey, announced that he was planning a multiyear, phased retirement. His plan was to decline new clients and reduce the number of classes as attrition cut into his base. His announcement happened to correspond with an accumulation of changes for me and the publishing industry.

The short version is: my backside was really tired of being sat upon for 40 or so hours a week, and the publishing industry's ongoing turmoil was making my freelance writing and editing work a less reliable source of income. I was ready for a change and ready to get out of my chair.

But what could I do that didn't involve much sitting? When I thought about things that I enjoyed doing and was reasonably proficient at, weightlifting rose to the top. And with Loren looking toward retirement, I knew there would be people wanting the program he offered. I spoke to him about it, and with his encouragement and advice, I took the USA Weightlifting Level 1 coach training and began putting the pieces of a business together: location, equipment, marketing. I'd put a business together before (a weekly newspaper) and previously I'd been a newspaper reporter writing about small business, so I had some idea of how to proceed.

Give Me Strength was born. The business was a good move for me, and it's been good for my clients. I started with three classes and many openings and now, six years later, I have seven classes and a waiting list, plus another coach is leading two classes in my space. This book lays out the process that got us here and the weightlifting program I use, which is pretty much Loren's program.

WHY IT CAN WORK FOR YOU

One thing I have come to understand over the years is just how rare this mode of exercise is in the public marketplace, especially for women and older adults. Most big gyms offer weight rooms with a full range of dumbbells and some have barbells, but you probably have to have a personal trainer to learn how to use them, and many if not most people can't afford one-on-one personal training.

The classes most gyms offer rarely give good, close instruction on lifting technique, or they don't go heavy. Many people either don't stick with lifting classes or wind up on machines. Machines have their place, but they're boring and don't provide functional strength the way weightlifting does.

Meanwhile, CrossFit has brought weightlifting to the attention of a wider audience, but many people are intimidated or simply uninterested in what one devotee called a "punishingly exhausting sweatfest."[1] And while some 60-year-olds may enjoy CrossFit, I'd venture that it's not for most of them. It's also not for lots of other people.

What's left for someone wanting to get strong? Small-class weightlifting workouts taught by you, me, and anyone else who appreciates weightlifting and is eager to share its benefits. Although physical limitations can rule out weightlifting for a few people, most can do it, perhaps with some accommodations. That's one of the great things about weightlifting: it can be adapted to a huge range of limitations.

So how about it? Are you ready to give weightlifting and its strength-building exercises a try? Ready to start your own business or expand your existing one? Then read on. There's a whole market out there waiting for you.

-II——II-

CHAPTER 1

YOUR PROSPECTIVE CLIENTS NEED YOU

Countless times, clients have asked me, "Do you know anybody who does something like this in [city name]?" The answer is always "no." A few times, I've tried to help out by doing internet searches using not only general search terms but also searching profiles of members of the National Strength and Conditioning Association and USA Weightlifting. Once or twice I found individuals or gyms that seemed to have some limited programming of the general kind I describe in this book, but that's about it.

It's entirely possible that other people are offering similar programs but they don't make themselves easy to find. If that's the case, it's probably for the same reason that I've been accused of having a "hidden gym." I have a thriving business and I don't need to do much in the way of advertising or other promotion. The same goes for my original weightlifting coach, who is doing a phased retirement of his business (operated out of his garage) after about 20 years.

These experiences should tell you something: that people like, benefit from, and seek out the kind of weightlifting experience I give them, but not enough people have access to that kind of coaching. I'd like to change that, because I have come to believe that weightlifting provides a profound benefit for daily life that grows ever more important as people get older. Meanwhile, I get the impression that most trainer or coach jobs can be frustrating in terms of income potential and autonomy.

With this book, I hope to encourage a business model that will address the needs both of adults trying to gain strength and coaches seeking real job satisfaction while making a decent living. Although my business is modest, it's satisfying as I watch clients get strong—and as I witness bigger, fancier, high-profile gyms go under with their major debt load and the steady churn of clientele.

So, if you like the idea of being your own boss and of making a real difference in the lives of people you serve, then read on. And if it resonates with you, then go for it! Chances are your business won't be identical to mine except, I hope, in the important ways: helping adults get strong through an effective and efficient exercise mode, and fulfilling your professional goals.

GET STARTED

Do you want a squad of faithful clients? How about the satisfaction of seeing your clients get stronger? Or hearing those clients report the ways their lives have improved since they started working with you? Or maybe you'd like to spend your time teaching and coaching instead of marketing?

If so, I can show you a system to achieve those goals. It's both revolutionary and as old as the first modern Olympics in 1896. It requires no fancy technology, no particularly expensive equipment, and it's suitable for people of nearly all sizes and ages. "It" is the adaptation of exercises and techniques of weightlifting to build strength and power and functional strength, while providing an abundance of ancillary benefits. And when I say weightlifting, I mean the activity that you've seen in the Olympics, but more on that later.

Further, this book also will show you how to start and grow a business using that weightlifting instruction as its basis, particularly when the instruction and your marketing is directed at mature adults, the people who have figured out that being strong is about feeling good and living well.

This chapter gives an overview of what this program and business model is about.

SMALL CLASSES

This program is more than just a set of exercises. This approach takes advantage of the social and motivational benefits of small classes. It's a different model from what is commonly seen at many gyms, where people sign up and don't show up. Or show up and get frustrated because equipment is unavailable or the class is too crowded. It's also different from the one-on-one approach of personal training, which can leave trainers shortchanged if clients cancel and which is financially out of reach, at least on a regular basis, for many if not most potential clients. These factors no doubt contribute to the relatively low pay of many gym employees.

Instead, take a highly effective strength-training regimen, add esprit de corps, and eliminate elements that irritate mature clients of all ages. (That means skip the ear-splitting music and walls of mirrors—two matters that multiple clients have commented on as a major appeal of my classes.) Put another way, provide an effective strength-building program that's inviting to people who feel out of place in a room full of mostly young men checking out their muscles in mirrors.

The result? Clients attend regularly and return class after class, year after year. Conversely, about two-thirds of gym members never use their gyms.[2] And health clubs typically lose 30% to 50% of their members every year![3] In my first session of this year, more than 92% of clients were renewing clients, and the "new" people joining the session were former clients. Here's more evidence of client loyalty: more than a quarter of my clients have been with me more than four years, which is more people than I started out with almost six years ago!

GROWN-UP CLIENTS

Meanwhile, it's probably not a coincidence that the average age of my clients is considerably in excess of the average gym member age of 40,[4] and that's another "revolutionary" aspect of this program. Although I have clients from the teens to eighties, more than 60% are in their fifties and sixties and almost 20% more are in their seventies. The remaining 20% are mostly in their thirties and forties but also include two in their eighties and a teenager. One more thing: more than 90% of my clients are women, and that's not just because I'm a woman. My first coach, the man who is the real developer of this program, wound up with a mostly female clientele. Women want and need strength as much as men, but they say they don't get what they need at gyms.

Of course, maybe those mature, active adults aren't really the demographic you had in mind when you decided to become a personal trainer or a coach. However, one interesting thing about my clients, regardless of their age, is that they're working out to feel better and to function better. No one is there just for appearance's sake; looking better is the bonus. Yes, if they stick with this program, their bodies will get stronger and leaner, and their improved fitness, strength, posture, and confidence surely will improve how they look. But because they're there for wellness reasons—and not to impress anybody or to lose weight for the beach/ Christmas formal/ wedding/class reunion—they have realistic expectations.

They know that "body sculpting" isn't likely to happen outside the surgery suite. If anything, this program tends to beat people's expectations.

My business does one thing—it teaches strength through weightlifting—but it does so in a way that gives clients more, something they tell me they don't get in other gyms: respect and a comfortable environment. That makes them, and me, happy and keeps me in business. You can do that, too.

FILLING A NEED, CHANGING LIVES

The shortcomings of current offerings in your community are probably similar to those in mine. Those deficiencies provide an opportunity for you to change people's lives for the better. Good weightlifting instruction provides a truly life-enhancing experience for clients—even more so than other modes of exercise. You, meanwhile, will reap considerable satisfaction from seeing your clients get stronger and from hearing the stories they tell about their new, stronger lives.

From what clients tell me, they frequently get inadequate attention, insufficient challenge, or too much of a push (that is, they get injured) when they have tried strength training elsewhere. Perhaps some professionals underestimate the potential strength of women and older clients. Perhaps trainers operate under an abundance of caution. Maybe they are fairly young and don't have much experience with older adults and therefore haven't seen what they are capable of, but I assure you they are capable of plenty if they have the right instruction and lift consistently. Nevertheless, you may find some differences between older and younger clients. Older clients may need to progress more slowly than young ones and show up with decades of wear and tear, but that's just fine as long as you, the coach, understand that.

Let me give you a few examples of the ways lives have changed among my clients:

- Roberta started lifting at age 48 and reports that within two months she was able to stop taking medication for arthritis in her back. She's now lifting remarkably heavy weights and loving feeling strong.

- Carol was 75 when she started lifting. She walked regularly and had been doing some kind of strength training through a local hospital fitness program for 10 years, but she felt as if it was no longer benefitting her. A woman of slight figure, she couldn't lift 15 pounds over her head or squat to pick things up. Now she can put her own carry-on case in a plane's overhead bin (when other passengers will let her, she says) and can squat to get books off the bottom shelf when she volunteers at the library. A bonus: her latest scan showed a remarkable increase in bone mineral density in her spine. That's huge.

- Diane had spent decades hunched over a keyboard before she started lifting at age 60. She says her strength increased, and the class has been "the best antidepressant" she's experienced. (There's research to confirm that she isn't exceptional in this respect.)

- Nancy was about 60 and had long been active. A painful hip, however, meant running and calisthenics no longer felt good and led her to try lifting. A year or two later, she had hip replacement surgery. She credits weightlifting beforehand with helping her recover quickly and well from the surgery. And, yes, she resumed lifting after surgery.

Each individual's experience may be slightly different depending on his or her native athletic abilities and starting strength, but the people mentioned above are in no way outliers. An outlier would be the 81-year-old client I had, a man who deeply squatted a decent amount of weight with excellent form, or the petite 62-year-old woman who squatted 120% of her body weight for repetitions.

I have countless reports from clients of an end to their back pain (especially from desk sitters) or knee pain and of generally being able to do the things they want to do to live fully in their gardens, with their grandchildren, and in their daily lives. I have clients who have artificial knees, artificial hips, unhappy shoulders, surgically reconstructed joints of various kinds, arthritic wrists and elbows and knees—and they have all benefited.

True, we have to make adaptations here and there, but that's one of the great things about barbell (and occasionally dumbbell) lifting versus machines; we can alter the way we do an exercise with more options than possible on a machine. Maybe Jane Doe's or John Roe's form isn't exactly like what you'd see among young, top-level competitive weightlifters, but so what? As long as they are lifting safely and getting the physical and mental benefits of weightlifting, who cares?

WHY WEIGHTLIFTING?

With so many options for resistance training, you may wonder why to choose weightlifting as the basis for your strength program. The reasons are several, as weightlifting has advantages that other modes of strength training can't match.

It's adjustable to each person's size and strength. Someone is 220 pounds and 5-foot-6? Or maybe 98 pounds and 5-foot-0? That's fine. They can probably lift weights. Same for the guy who is 6-foot-7 and 220 pounds. Every person may not be able to make every move, or at least not without some modifications, but darned near everybody can lift weights. You don't have to worry that they are too small or too big to fit well on a machine. It's OK if they have long arms or short arms. If they want to lift, it can probably be arranged.

It requires skill. This is an advantage because it keeps the lifting interesting—your clients can and will get better with practice—and it uses their brains more than doing simple, one-joint moves on a machine.

It teaches form that you can apply in daily life. Your clients can use their deadlift technique when lifting a piece of heavy equipment. They can use your squatting technique to save their backs as they pick up (or put down) their kindergartener or aged dog. No one is going to learn that on a leg-press apparatus.

It boosts balance. Although my weightlifting workouts typically don't have a specific balance component, lifters get balance practice with every lift. That's because they are lifting heavy things with their bodies in space. Mostly unconsciously, the body is constantly making tiny adjustments to make a person stay upright as he or she lifts, aiding the ability to sense and counteract shifting demands on the musculoskeletal system.

It's fun. No, really! It's fun to learn new skills, to apply them in daily life, and to work with others while doing so.

It promotes quickness. Did you know weightlifters are the quickest athletes at the Olympics? Well, that's what weightlifting coaches will tell you, and weightlifters have to be superfast to sling massive weights overhead. Even though your clients aren't lifting world-class loads, the moves they learn through weightlifting can help to maintain their quickness by using fast-twitch muscle fibers (which dwindle at a faster rate than their companion slow-twitch fibers).

That can be very helpful in recreational sports—and for keeping your clients from falling down if they trip.

It promotes flexibility and fuller range of motion. Unless someone is extremely flexible going in, she is likely to increase flexibility and range of motion in the big joints (shoulder, hips, knees, ankles) through weightlifting.

It's efficient. What other exercise program do you know that will strengthen all your major muscle groups in just two hours a week, give or take? Barbell exercise provides that efficiency.

WHY IT MATTERS

Stronger is better. No, not for bragging rights, but for living fully. With greater strength comes greater capacity for such satisfying activities as picking up grandchildren, bags of garden mulch, or cases of wine—as well as for the mundane, such as getting out of a chair! These are the kinds of activity that gradually become difficult if not impossible as people age, and they are the kinds of activity that you can help clients reclaim. If someone does want bragging rights, of course, that's within the realm of possibility, too. Weightlifting simply has many advantages over other kinds of strength training to achieve those real-world gains.

People often take their strength for granted, but unless they do something to stay strong, ordinary daily life has its way with muscles, starting in your thirties. Few of us notice at first, but the 3% to 5% muscle loss per decade adds up and increases later in life. In fact, typically by age 60, people have lost 20% to 40% of their muscle strength.[5] The loss is gradual, but somewhere along the line your potential clients might notice themselves reaching for the edge of the dinner table to help get up after a meal. Or they may find that they prefer riding in an SUV because it's easier to get in and out of than a lower-to-the-ground vehicle. And their groceries just keep getting heavier. Meanwhile, people lose bone mass along with muscle. This problem is particularly true for postmenopausal women.

The big picture indicates that being stronger in general keeps people healthier. Or, as a government report drily puts it, "Evidence indicates that the preservation of fat-free mass and, in particular, skeletal muscle mass is associated with favorable health outcomes with advancing age."[6]

Strength training is the solution, and it's something that all adults need to do. Indeed, it's part of the activity guidelines for Americans issued by the U.S. Department of Health and Human Services. The kind of strength training program this book describes works not only because it gets people strong, but also because it keeps them coming back, both to your and their benefit.

NOTICEABLE IMPROVEMENTS

Although part of my clients' persistence and loyalty no doubt is due to my charm and good looks, the main reason they stay is that they can see and feel and measure their improvements while getting the support of their coach and classmates.

As I said, I didn't invent this model; it very closely hews to the method used by my first weightlifting coach, Loren McVey. It worked for me as a novice and now as an experienced lifter, and it has worked for me as a coach and business owner. The real reason for Loren's and my success is that this program gives people what they want and need, and they tell their friends. Beyond business cards and a web presence, my business has never advertised because it hasn't needed to.

This book aims to get similar success for you and your clients. It will explain the program and guide you in starting a similar program. If you love the idea of having faithful clients, rewarding work, and a focus on helping people get strong, then it's time to get started. But first, you need to know how to teach them to do so. That's the subject of the next chapter.

GET TRAINED

The first step in starting or expanding your weight-training business is in getting trained yourself, because you need to have a thorough understanding and appreciation of how to lift weights and how to pass on that knowledge. This chapter covers your training and introduces the workouts that you will be using with your clients.

LEARNING TO LIFT

If you already know how to lift with good form, then you probably can skip this section, but if you aren't sure, read on. Chances are your exposure to lifting is limited, because weightlifting remains an obscure sport in the United States.

Although I don't necessarily believe that a person has to be an expert at a given sport to be able to coach it, you will benefit in multiple ways if you do learn to lift and learn it with a good coach. You will lift better when you do and will gain knowledge in how to teach the lifts, particularly the clean-and-jerk or the power clean and power jerk or push press. (The power clean and push press are key elements of the weightlifting program that we'll detail in this book.)

The trick is in finding a good coach. Indeed, finding a coach may well be the trickiest part of this whole program, as it isn't always easy to find well-qualified weightlifting coaches, and when you do find one he or she probably will be geared more toward training competitive athletes. That fact will benefit you when you want to teach weightlifting, but when you want to learn it can be a problem. Two widely available programs, CrossFit and Les Mills's Bodypump, use some Olympic lifts or variations. Multiple people have told me, however, that they got little in the way of detailed or personal instruction on the lifts in these workouts. As a result, I'd recommend seeking a coach in one of these ways:

USA Weightlifting. This organization oversees weightlifting competitions in the United States, and it maintains a directory of coaches who have taken and passed its certification programs. You can search its directory by location and

find it at https://www.teamusa.org/usa-weightlifting/coaching/coach-directory.
Because USA Weightlifting is competition-oriented, these coaches may or may
not be willing to work with you if you aren't interested in competing.

Nearby universities. If you live near a university with a physical education or
athletic training program, check out whether it has a program to teach weightlifting, or give the school's offices a call to see whether they can point you to
someone who can teach you.

NSCA. The National Strength and Conditioning Association provides a program
for Certified Strength and Conditioning Specialists. If you see a trainer with CSCS
after his or her name, that means they've earned that certification. You can search
for a CSCS trainer near you at http://customer.usreps.org. The NSCA certification
is mostly a book learnin' program, however, so if you seek a trainer through the
NSCA, be sure to ask questions about that person's weightlifting experience.

Local gyms. You can seek a personal trainer who has experience in weightlifting
through local gyms. Just because someone is qualified as a personal trainer
doesn't mean he or she knows how to do weightlifting, though. The reverse is
also true; someone can know weightlifting without being a personal trainer.
So ask details about their weightlifting experience. Tell them you want to know
how to do a power clean or clean-and-jerk.

Different kinds of strength training

This program uses weightlifting as its basis, but it's helpful to be aware of
other types of strength training to avoid confusion. Here is an overview of
some terms and types of strength training.

Strength training or resistance training. These are general terms for
building muscle strength by contracting muscles to oppose some external
resistance. Could be weightlifting, yes, but also body-weight training
(push-ups being a familiar example), working with elastic bands, or
weight machines.

Weight training. This general term applies to strength training using
machines or free weights. Free weights, incidentally, include any weight

that isn't attached to some kind of apparatus. Among them are barbells—the big, long bars—and dumbbells, which some clients know as "hand weights," as well as kettlebells.

Olympic-style weightlifting (or simply weightlifting). Weightlifting is a competitive sport involving two lifts, the snatch and the clean-and-jerk. Weightlifting employs strength, power, and flexibility. Technique is crucial to successful weightlifting.

Bodybuilding. A combination of strength training and diet, bodybuilding aims to maximize muscle size, definition, and symmetry. Appearance is the focus.

Powerlifting. This competitive sport encompasses three lifts: the squat, bench press, and deadlift. The term is a misnomer, as power implies the combination of strength and speed, and these lifts are all about strength. They involve shorter movement of weights than Olympic-style weightlifting.

LEARNING TO COACH WEIGHTLIFTING

The key lifts that distinguish weightlifting—the clean-and-jerk and the snatch—are complicated. Good technique is critical to successful lifts. You will gain knowledge of those techniques as you learn to lift. That experience will help you to understand the instruction you get when you take a weightlifting coaching course.

Even if you have a degree in exercise science or exercise physiology, chances are your exposure to the Olympic lifts was limited. USA Weightlifting lists only three college courses in Olympic lifting,[7] but the list doubtless isn't comprehensive. Only a handful of colleges and universities maintain intercollegiate lifting programs, although a couple of dozen or so have weightlifting clubs.[8] Consequently, your best bet is to take a coaching course through USA Weightlifting.

The two-day USAW Level 1 coaching course, called Sports Performance Coach, gives a basic introduction to coaching the Olympic lifts. That includes the competition lifts and associated lifts—such as power snatch, power clean, and power jerk—as well as very basic instruction regarding programming and the rules of competition. The instructors are very knowledgeable, but be advised that there's more to learn than you can pick up in one weekend (and another reason why you will do well to learn to lift from a good coach). Courses are offered at various locations throughout the year. You can find them at https://webpoint. usaweightlifting.org/wp15/Events2/Events.wp?evtc_CategoryGroup=Course. The Level 2 course, Advanced Sports Performance, gives further instruction in the same topics plus information about biomechanics, physiology, coaching, competition, and more.

IF YOU CAN

Having learned to lift and taken the initial USAW training, you have acquired the minimum knowledge to undertake the course this book describes. If you can, try to find a competition you can watch, including any level from youth to master's, so that you can see a lot of lifting before you start coaching. You will learn as you go along, but take advantage of any opportunities you have to observe. Although the program in this book doesn't include the snatch, it does use the power clean and the push press (similar to a power jerk), and the lifts use very quick movements. We'll talk more here about what to watch for, but it's good to practice watching.

THE WORKOUTS YOU WILL LEAD

The specific lifts that we use in this weightlifting program are strength-building and skill-building lifts that competitive weightlifters use to prepare for the competition lifts. Hence, you need to know how to do them and to teach them. The lifts:

- Power clean
- Push press (front of neck)
- Squats
- Romanian deadlift
- Bench press
- Bent-over-row
- Core exercises

If you consider this list, you will realize that these exercises provide for strengthening of all the major muscle groups and in a balanced way, so that you avoid problems such as rounded shoulders from too much bench pressing and not enough strengthening of the back. You can add supplementary lifts if desired to work on smaller muscles, such as in the lower leg and forearm.

The USAW training probably will not teach you how to do all these lifts. If you don't know all of them, make sure you learn from your own coach or trainer.

WHAT NEXT?

Naturally, knowing how to lift and how to teach lifting is only the beginning to starting your own weightlifting business. The next chapters present a guide to getting your business or program started. The text assumes that you want to start your own business, but the ideas are applicable to running a program in an existing gym. Read and use what you need, and then get out there and help people get strong!

CHAPTER 3

THE BUSINESS END

As much as you may believe in and want to pursue weightlifting instruction and coaching, it's important to consider the business management aspects before you go too far. You may want to create a business plan. Scores of books have been published that tell you how to write a business plan. It's generally a good idea, especially if you have never run a business, and it may be required if you need to borrow money to start. Still, I don't know that a written plan is necessary (I didn't do it, but I'd been self-employed a long time), but you definitely need to know what your costs and revenue are likely to be before you jump in.

Most of the discussion in this chapter assumes that you are starting from scratch as an independent business operator. The end of the chapter includes a brief discussion of other business models.

GETTING STARTUP INFORMATION

In addition to this book, read a general book or two on how to start a business. It will cover such topics as legal business structure (sole proprietorship? limited liability corporation? another type of corporation?) and finances. There are plenty of books at the library, or start with the U.S. Small Business Administration's guide at https://www.sba.gov/starting-business/. Then, use the information in this chapter to guide you as you answer the questions, especially the money questions, that the books or websites pose.

In addition, the SBA partners with universities across the United States and U.S. territories to operate Small Business Development Centers. These centers provide various services and training opportunities for prospective business owners. You can find one in your state at https://www.sba.gov/tools/local-assistance/sbdc.

STARTING SMALL

Starting up with a big operation isn't necessary, and I'm not even sure it's desirable.

By starting small and building, you can minimize your startup costs, learn what works best for you and your clients, and allow word-of-mouth to build your clientele. Unless you already have a big and loyal following—or don't mind losing money for quite a while—starting small is a good way to test the market as well as your ability and desire to manage a business. Plus, starting small allows you to continue to earn money through other endeavors to keep you in groceries as you build the business. That's what I did, and I'm very glad about it. My business grew slowly and steadily, and I never had to go into debt. I also didn't lose my mind (or too many clients) because I was in over my head financially or organizationally.

Costs and revenue, as detailed in the next sections, will vary widely depending on your market. Still, as gyms go, this approach has relatively low startup costs. When looking at the money, make the most realistic estimates you can, then worst- and best-case scenarios. Or at least take your "realistic" estimate and do calculations that assume your expenses will be 20% higher and your revenues will be 20% lower.

REVENUE

So what kind of revenue can you expect? It's highly dependent on your local market, but a good guideline is to consider how much the typical or upscale local gyms cost on a monthly basis. You can reasonably hope to charge a fee that correlates to about that much per person per month. In other words, if ABC Gym charges $100 a month, you probably can, too.

If a potential client asks you to justify that fee, noting that you don't have the range of facilities and classes available at ABC Gym, point out that you offer something ABC Gym doesn't: small classes, personal instruction, and guidance on an ongoing basis. And no crowds or waiting for equipment or other inconveniences and annoyances of big gyms. Another way to look at it: your client can figure what it would cost to have (or even share) a personal trainer twice a week and determine what a good value you offer.

If you have the time and inclination, you can add to your revenue by selling related products, such as nutritional supplements, T-shirts, and so forth. Unless you go with some high-markup supplements that you can persuade people to buy on an ongoing basis (not something I am interested in doing), your ancillary revenue probably will be minimal. I sell chilled, bottled water and some snacks (healthy snack bars) at low markup, primarily for the convenience of my clients. We have done T-shirts but, again, sold them essentially at cost. Another revenue possibility includes offering one-on-one sessions in addition to classes.

The main way you will increase revenue, though, is to add clients and classes.

COSTS

Here's a breakdown of costs you are likely to incur:

- Startup costs
- Rent
- Utilities
- Insurance
- Equipment
- Supplies
- Licenses, fees, memberships, dues, subscriptions
- Other

Let's take a look at them one by one.

Startup costs. These are largely one-time expenses (or once plus a little maintenance) that you may need to get up and running, such as legal fees if you decide to incorporate or accountant fees if you need help setting up a record-keeping system.

Rent. Rent is my single biggest expense, but it wasn't for my first nine months in operation. My business started in a space I used for free in a building a friend owned and wasn't using. It was far from ideal. The cooling was inadequate, and it had only space heaters. The floor was wavy. But it had a roof and plentiful natural light. And it was free. Loren has operated his business for 20 years, give or take, out of his double garage. It's a bit cramped. Roll-out trash containers are parked there beside a giant bag of bird seed. The natural light is nonexistent, except when he opens the garage door from time to time. But it's his garage.

It came with the house! Yes, he added a heating and cooling unit and more lights than he probably would have had otherwise, but that's it for the space.

The point, clearly, is that if you can find somewhere to get started rent-free, then take it. Look at all the swank gyms that have gone out of business. We want yours to survive and prosper, so at least in the beginning try to keep costs down. The next chapter will guide you in terms of what to look for in a location. If you have to rent a space, then do it, but if you can get rolling for free, then do that!

Utilities. This expense will depend on your space. Ask your prospective landlord what kind of utility fees you are likely to incur. Assume that you will want to keep the ambient temperature on the cool side. Young, macho types may enjoy maximizing sweat, but few others do, particularly in our demographic. In fact, I've had prospective clients ask explicitly if the workouts will make them sweat! The answer is highly individual, of course, but if you live in a climate that gets above, say, 75 degrees F, your clients will want air-conditioning. And don't expect them to be enthusiastic about lifting if the temperature is much below 60 degrees.

Insurance. Insurance is generally regulated by states, so what is required and what is available may vary from one place to another. Chances are, though, you will want general business liability insurance, providing coverage for such things as tripping accidents or, say, you drop a barbell on your client's phone; commercial property coverage (that is, renter's insurance for your business to cover losses due to fire, for example); and your own health insurance. You may be able to get, or at least get a price for, liability insurance if you are a member of NSCA or another fitness organization. Otherwise, you will need to call agents for commercial insurance carriers for prices.

Equipment. The basic setup for the plan in this book requires three lifting platforms, each including a power rack and wood blocks for doing cleans without bumper plates; lifting bars; weight plates; dumbbells; and trash receptacles. You might also want a chalkboard or whiteboard, a bulletin board, a clock, cubbies for clients' use, coat hooks, or hangers. Chapter 6 provides equipment and supplies details.

Supplies. Depending on your setup, you are likely to need or want a first-aid kit, a couple of bar cushions, lifting straps, hand sanitizer, and trash bags. Maybe chalk.

Licenses, fees, memberships, dues, subscriptions. These items may or may not be optional, depending on your local laws and regulations:

• Possibly required. Check with the city and/or state offices in your location that oversee business operations. You may have to pay assorted governmental fees, such as to register your business, occupy your facility, or get the permission to undertake any number of other related activities. These fees fall into the general business startup category, which this book does not address in detail.

• Probably optional. You may want to join the NSCA, the National Academy of Sports Medicine, or other such organization for whatever insurance, information, and continuing education options they may offer. You had to join USA Weightlifting to take its training course, and you may or may not want to maintain your membership. These organizations have publications associated with them, which likely will satisfy most of your information needs. Other periodicals seem geared to bodybuilding, which is not our interest.

OTHER CONCERNS

An inescapable aspect of running a business is running a business. By running a business, I mean that in addition to doing the coaching and keeping track of your clients, you also need to market yourself and manage other essential business tasks, such as:

- ask for and collect money;
- pay the bills;
- keep financial records for tax purposes;
- buy supplies; and
- undertake or hire out tasks such as cleaning.

If you love working with people and helping them get strong, that's wonderful! If you can't tolerate or lack the skills to do the "paperwork" and other duties, then you probably need a partner who can and will handle those, or you need to undertake the exercise part of this program with clients at someone else's gym or other facility. I would love it if you would do it somewhere, as I wish more people could take advantage of this kind of weightlifting program!

Whatever "business model" you choose, I am thrilled that you are looking to develop a weightlifting program to help adults gain and maintain strength! The need for programs that build significant strength for women and for adults ages 50 and older is huge and growing. When you work with them, both you and they will benefit. If you are ready to proceed, the next chapters get into the nitty-gritty.

CHAPTER 4

PLAN YOUR PROGRAM

This program is based on time-tested exercises that build muscle strength, coordination, flexibility, and bones. It is a simple program of barbell and core exercises—so simple, in fact, that when I first heard about it, I thought it sounded boring. Turns out, though, that critical aspects of the program keep it interesting and keep clients motivated and coming back. Those aspects are the lifting program itself and the social aspect.

This chapter gives an overview of a typical workout and an introduction and sampling of periodized workouts. It reviews why we do each lift and details some common errors to watch for as well as adaptations you can offer your clients. Then we will discuss core exercises.

Here's the simple part of the program. Your clients will learn and perform six lifts: power clean, push press, squats, Romanian deadlifts, bench press, and bent-over rows. After learning the technique and establishing a calculated 1-repetition maximum (1RM), lifters then move to a form of periodization to build further strength. Volume and intensity of the lifts change periodically also to encourage the body and muscles to continually be in an adaptation mode. Workouts occur twice a week, and each workout, which usually can be completed in an hour or so, addresses all the major muscle groups. That's an efficient workout.

Lifters like this approach because they like being challenged—and they like getting a break from time to time. Certainly, some people always want to go full bore; those people are more likely to get injured or to suffer the frustrations of overtraining. I have a few clients who have that tendency but they have come to appreciate the benefits of taking a more measured approach. I don't recall anyone dropping out because the program wasn't challenging enough.

Lifters also like the program because they can see quantifiable changes and set quantifiable goals through occasional resetting of the 1RM. In addition, of course, are the benefits they see and feel in their everyday lives.

Remember, this program isn't intended to train competitive athletes; it's intended to improve the health, strength, and quality of life for your clients, many (if not most) who will bring the remainders of past accidents, injuries, and other insults to the body that happen over time. Also, this book is not intended to be your primary source of instruction on how to do any of these lifts. If you don't already know how to do them, get some in-person instruction from an experienced coach.

BIG PICTURE

Classes meet twice a week, with a day or two between workouts. Because each workout addresses all the major muscle groups, there are no "upper body days" or "leg days," and a minimum of a day between workouts is essential to allow for recovery. I have classes that meet Monday–Wednesday and Tuesday–Thursday. On weeks when workouts are especially heavy, a Monday–Thursday and Tuesday–Friday rotation probably would be better, but that doesn't seem to work for many people's schedules. (I've asked.)

To the extent that you can, encourage clients to be as consistent in attending as possible. Consistency leads to results. As my coach noted (more or less), you wouldn't expect your teeth to stay healthy if you only brushed them once a week, and you can't expect your muscles to stay healthy if you only work to maintain them once a week (or less). Research indicates that you need to work out twice a week to gain and maintain strength.

Order of battle

Each workout follows this pattern:

EXERCISE	WHY WE DO IT
Warmup	Prepare for lifting
Power clean	Promote quickness, coordination
Push press	Promote quickness, coordination, shoulder strength
Squat	Strengthen quadriceps, hamstrings, glutes, back
Romanian deadlift (RDL)	Strengthen hamstrings, glutes, back

Bench press	Strengthen pectorals, biceps, triceps
Bent-over row	Strengthen back, biceps, triceps
Core work/abdominal exercises	Strengthen abdominals, back

Following is a description of each segment of the workout.

Big-picture coaching cues

You may know some actions so well that you could forget that your clients don't! So remember that these tips apply to every lift:

- Get good position set for every repetition.

- Take a breath for every repetition (and exhale on effort).

- Brace core for every repetition.

- Focus your eyes on a spot straight ahead for every repetition.

- Pay attention to where your body (and its various parts) is and how it feels for every repetition.

- And for almost every lift, a "good position" involves shoulders retracted and down, core tight, and butt out.

Warm-up

As with any exercise program, you should start with a general warm-up to raise the body temperature and get blood flowing to the extremities. Suggestions are two or more minutes walking, marching, or running in place, using a stationary bicycle, dancing, or similar activity.

A specific warm-up follows the general to prime the muscles, the joints, and the nervous system for the exercises to follow. Suggested specific warm-ups, each for 10–12 repetitions:

Up-and-down. Stand and hold light bar in front of chest with hands at about shoulder width. Reach overhead, then—keeping bar close to body and knees soft—reach to ankles. Keep back flat.

Good morning. Place light bar on shoulders while standing. With knees soft and the back flat, bend from hip until torso is about parallel to floor, then stand back up.

Squat. Using light bar, squat in the normal squatting pattern.

"Light bar," by the way, will vary according to the strength of the lifter. For older, novice lifters, a broomstick may suffice. As people get stronger, they should advance to progressively heavier bars, but never heavy enough that the warm-up feels like work.

Power clean

We do the power clean first in the workouts because it's the most complicated, and because the nervous system gets tired faster than the muscles. I teach it following the mode suggested by USA Weightlifting (starting from the hang), although I have seen other approaches.

Power clean is the most challenging and, for different clients, either the most frustrating or the most satisfying of our lifts. For you, it likely will be both the most challenging and the most satisfying lift to teach because it's a complex movement, but its benefits are worth it.

- Remind your client that this lift has many moving parts, and many people take months to get the hang of it.

- Focus on only one or two aspects of the lift at a time. Doing more overwhelms or confuses people.

- Remind your client that the power in this lift comes from the legs; if she tries to do it all with her arms and back, she won't get far and could strain her back.

PROBLEM AREA	POSSIBLE MODIFICATION
Wrist, elbow, or shoulder	Perform clean pull, either permanently or until problems resolve
Hip, knee, or ankle	Clean from the hang or knee Push off without jumping
Feet	Push off without jumping

Push press

Like the power clean, this lift uses all the major muscle groups, although not as intensely. Start instruction with the overhead press (also known as a military press) only. Once the lifter is comfortable with that movement, add the "push" that comes from the legs.

This lift essentially is a simplified version of a power jerk. The differences are that in the push press the lifter makes the catch with straight legs (versus bent in the jerk) and that pressing out with the arms is acceptable in the push press. I learned to do the lift behind my neck but after several years and a shoulder impingement, I moved myself and, subsequently, new clients to performing the front-of-neck push press. In front of the neck keeps the shoulder in a more stable position and therefore reduces the chance of injury, although the rear deltoid gets less work. I encourage lifters to do a supplemental lift (known as bent-over lateral raises or rear deltoid flies, among other names) to give the rear deltoids a little more work.

- Aim for a shallow and quick "dip and drive." Many people seem inclined to go low and slow.

- Push off using the whole foot, not just the front of it.

- Encourage a full range of motion. That is, when arms are fully extended, retract bar overhead (but not painfully, of course) before returning to start.

PROBLEM AREA	POSSIBLE MODIFICATION
Knee pain	Push off with legs but don't jump or let feet fully leave floor
Shoulder pain or inflexibility	Keep elbows close to the trunk
	Keep arm and shoulder muscles engaged when returning to start position; use muscles as if pulling bar down

Incidentally, I have three clients at the moment who do power jerks. All three are quite athletic, and two of them started doing power jerks without realizing it when we added legs to the overhead press. The third asked to learn. I figure encouraging those power moves is all to the good.

Supplemental lift: lateral raise. Once clients are up to speed on the push press, start having them do lateral raises after their push presses. Watch for torso parallel to floor (or close), elbows bent, and upper arms moving approximately perpendicular to the torso.

Squats

Many exercise experts have opined that squats are the most important or most useful lift a person can do, and for good reason. Doing squats helps us maintain the ability to do many activities that allow and improve a high quality of life. These are the activities we take for granted—until we can't do them anymore. Examples include getting in and out of a chair or a car, going up and down steps, getting on and off the toilet (and urinary continence for that matter), getting items off the bottom shelf, picking up items off the floor. Even more important are the ability to avoid falling when you trip and picking yourself up if you do fall.

That said, squats are challenging at first for many people. When I started lifting at age 51, I was horrified to discover that I couldn't do a single bodyweight squat despite walking many miles a week. (Few people realize that walking and running won't maintain strength.) At 63, I can load a bar with more than my body weight and do deep squats for repetitions, a feat I wouldn't have imagined possible when I started.

The point is this: many if not most of your clients will struggle at first with squats. Problems will include flexibility and knee issues and, especially, lack of strength. Happily, many knee problems seem to resolve as the quadriceps, hamstrings, and gluteal muscles get stronger.

- Emphasize the importance of bracing the core. One cue seems to work for most people: brace your core as if you were about to take a punch in the stomach.

- Remind lifters to keep feet flat and to push into their heels when they rise.

- Place a stool or chair behind newbies to give them confidence they won't fall and to provide a target depth. As they get stronger, you can use a lower stool for the same reasons and eventually eliminate the stool.

PROBLEM AREA	POSSIBLE MODIFICATION
Knee pain	Adjust stance. The adjustment likely will differ from person to person, but try changing the distance between feet and/or the angle of toes.
	Recruit glutes. Activate glutes before squatting by doing some bridges or other glute-focused warm-ups. Then, during squat, press knees slightly outward.
	Try alternative squat, such as goblet squat or step-ups.
Ankle inflexibility	Elevate heels. Try placing thin (about 1/4-inch) plates under heels. Weightlifting shoes help, too.
	Perform flexibility work.

Romanian deadlift

The Romanian deadlift (RDL) seems like such a simple movement that it surprises me how many people have difficulty performing it properly. Once they do, however, they tend to like it, as they typically can lift more weight with the RDL than with any other lift. That's not why we do it, of course, but it's great when clients feel successful.

It's also a lift that many clients initially fear. Here's why: the most common complaints among new clients are lower back pain and knee problems. Unsurprisingly, much of their pain or discomfort is associated with low muscle strength; happily, greater strength significantly improves both those conditions. Consequently, you need to be sure to progress slowly with the RDL both to gradually increase back strength and to gradually increase client confidence.

There seem to be multiple notions of what constitutes an RDL. The version I teach starts with the bar at the thighs, with knees very slightly bent. The lifter moves hips rearward and, hinging from the hips, slides the bar down the front of the legs until the lower back is approximately parallel to the floor. The lifter then pulls hips forward and raises the bar to the starting position. The back needs to stay flat (or very slightly extended) the entire move.

Most people catch on to this lift readily, but those who don't really seem to struggle to get it. They want to use their arms to lift the bar, or they turn it into a bent-over squat, for example. Be sure to start very light and make sure the form is right before adding weight.

● Watch the back. It's crucial that the back stays flat or slightly extended with shoulder blades together and down. You know that, of course, but you may be amazed to see people try to do this lift primarily by flexing the spine. Yikes! In addition, some people (especially those with lots of hamstring flexibility) may keep the back flat to a certain point and then let the lumbar spine start to flex; remind them not to go too low and thereby strain the lower back.

● Watch the knees. Increasing the knee bend is probably the most frequent error/cheat I see in the RDL. Although increased bend isn't dangerous, it does unload the hamstrings, which defeats a key purpose of the lift.

● Cue "butt out, weight toward heels." The people who struggle with the technique often seem unable to shift the hips back. A cue to shift their weight often helps. You may also need to remind these clients to keep the bar in contact with the body.

PROBLEM AREA	POSSIBLE MODIFICATION
Lower back	For most situations, no modification, just go slowly and increase gradually.
	Start with low-back/glute strengthening exercises such as bridges (with or without weight), donkey kicks, or kickbacks (with or without weight).
	Dumbbell one-leg deadlift.
Upper back	Usually only arises when weight gets very heavy, but remedy is same: brace shoulder blades in retracted and down position.
Weak grip	Use lifting straps. You may need to help clients a few times before they get the hang of using them.

Bench press

For reasons I can't explain, many people put a lot of stock in bench press. At some point, almost everyone who lifts is asked, "How much do you bench?" The reasonable answer is, "Who cares?" Unless you're a football lineman, the ability to push something away from your chest just isn't particularly important or valuable. Nevertheless, we do this lift as part of the workout to address all the major muscle groups.

This lift comes after the RDL so as to give the back a bit more rest before moving on to the bent-over row, but it's acceptable to trade the order of the bench press and the bent-over row if necessary or desirable due to equipment availability or, even, personal preference.

- Expect arms and the bar path to be wobbly at first. This issue corrects itself as lifters become more practiced with the lift.

- Encourage quick drive off the chest. As weight is added, the speed won't be visible, but by practicing quick and immediate direction reversal at the bottom of the eccentric portion, your clients will have greater success with the lift.

- Emphasize form to protect shoulders: upper arm at about 45 degrees from body; shoulder blades retracted, down and locked; grip width that provides for vertical forearm at bottom of lift.

PROBLEM AREA	POSSIBLE MODIFICATION
Lower back	If need be, place feet on extended legs of bench or on the top of the bench, instead of on the floor, to reduce discomfort from low back arch. Note, however, that lifter may lose a little side-to-side stability compared with feet on floor.
Upper back	Make sure shoulder blades are retracted and down (which, yes, will lift the chest), upper back muscles contracted.
Shoulders (even when using good form)	Reduce weight. Try dumbbell bench presses. Try decline bench presses.

Bent-over row

Bent-over rows seem to be among the easiest to teach and learn—but also among the least favorite (if not the least favorite) among the lifts. We do barbell rows (which give additional work to the hamstrings and lower back) rather than dumbbell rows except for some beginners who start with minimal low-back strength and for some other lifters with chronic low-back issues.

Suggest starting as if doing an RDL and stopping at the lowest point before letting the bar fall away from the body. Then pull elbows to ceiling with the bar traveling vertically. Failing to keep torso or at least the lumbar spine approximately parallel to the floor is the number one fault people make in my classes. This more upright position recruits more muscles, making the lift easier, but it reduces the amount of work for the lats, a key focus of this lift.

⊚ Watch the wrists. Many people flex their wrists as they try to bring the bar to their ribs. Besides potentially aggravating wrist and elbow problems with that move, it reduces the range of motion in the shoulders and reduces the work of the lats.

PROBLEM AREA	POSSIBLE MODIFICATION
Lower back	Go with dumbbell bent-over rows
Excess belly limiting range of motion	Go with dumbbell bent-over rows

Core work/abdominal exercises

We finish each workout with several core exercises. See Appendix B, at the end of the book, for a list. Different practitioners have different views about the approach and even about the benefit of doing core work. One view is that such exercise is unnecessary, as every lift works the core. Another view is that the core exercises reinforce and provide additional trunk strength for greater success in the lifts. I lean to the second point of view, although I don't lean so far as to do what I would consider to be extreme ab workouts.

Then there is the matter of which exercises for the core/abdominal muscles are best. At one extreme is the camp that would have you do pretty much nothing but plank-type exercises (the maximum-safety camp), and at the other extreme are those who go for maximum everything—extending, bending, and twisting your spine as much as possible (the gung-ho/macho camp) with added weight where possible.

I stand firmly on the fence. Because daily life for most people involves movement, I'm skeptical of core workouts that are almost exclusively static—that is, the maximum-safety approach. (And planks have their downsides, too.) I understand, however, that pushing your spine to its limits can push it too far. And, unfortunately, sometimes exercises that do the most for your abs also put your back at greater risk.

My response is to suggest a wide variety of core exercises, including some that are on the "avoid" list of the max-safety campers. At the same time, though, my clients have the option to substitute exercises as appropriate for their particular needs. The hope is that by going with variety helps minimize potential harm while maximizing the opportunities to work on all the core muscles. I remind clients to keep the lower back flat (while maintaining the lumbar curve), and modify lifts if necessary to avoid stressing the back. As with all exercise-related matters, the most important advice is for each person to listen to her or his body, keeping in mind the principle, if it hurts, don't do it. If it's just hard work, well, that's another story

STARTING NEW LIFTERS

Chances are most of your clients will have little lifting experience. A few may have some weightlifting background, but unless you've worked with them recently and you know their skill and strength level, go ahead and start them as if they're entirely new to lifting.

A typical progression for new clients follows this pattern:

1. Ask about any previous injuries or infirmities so that you can work around them as needed.

2. Start light and with relatively high repetitions. I typically have new people do 2 sets of 10 repetitions on each lift for the first day and go to 3 sets of 10 thereafter until they are up to speed with the technique.

3. After that, gradually add weight until it appears that the lifter is getting close to her limit or the form breaks down. Then, calculate a 1-repetition maximum (1RM) and start doing periodized workouts, as discussed on the following pages.

Watch carefully

There may be as much art as science in starting new lifters. Watch, listen, and use your experience to guide you in how fast to advance your clients.

Ask questions

It is a good practice to ask clients to complete a formal questionnaire about various health matters as well as musculoskeletal issues, or you might do something more informal, as I do. You can ask clients to complete the PAR-Q test (which has been replaced by the Get Active Questionnaire) and consult a physician if indicated. Links are in Appendix A, at the end of the book. I then ask clients about any particular concerns we need to take into consideration, such as complaints about joints. I modify lifts accordingly. I also ask them about their general level of activity and any strength-related work they may have done in the recent past. That information helps give me a sense of how to proceed.

Start light

How light is light? Naturally, it depends on the individual. What works for me is getting some sense of what kind of strength-building activities the person has been undertaking in the recent past and then give them a bar that is a little lighter than I might reasonably think she or he can handle. Provide instruction in the desired movement, and then ask the client to do it. With a little experience and by asking the client questions regarding effort and comfort or discomfort, you will have a good sense of a reasonable starting weight for the client.

Aim initially for weight that provides noticeable resistance but isn't difficult to move. Pay close attention to the amount of effort the client appears to require and how smoothly he or she is able to complete the movement. Ask the client whether it felt easy, felt like work, or was difficult to do. If it felt like work, but not difficult, then you probably have them at approximately the right amount of weight. If that isn't the case, change the amount of weight accordingly. When in doubt, go or stay lighter.

For the first few workouts it is especially important to check in often with clients, both during instruction and afterward, including at the next class session. Among the questions to ask:

- How did that feel?
- Does anything hurt?
- Do you have questions?

It's also helpful for you to look at their faces as well as their moves. Some people are reluctant to speak up, so if you see them wince and they tell you that nothing hurt, you might want to follow up and ask, "So what was that face about?"

You also may find it helpful to remember that different personalities may take markedly different approaches to weightlifting. I once had a client (sort of) who on the very first day while getting initial instruction announced, "I can't do this. I don't want to hurt myself." And that was that for her. She wasn't interested in trying the remaining lifts. She didn't care what the friend who referred her had said. She didn't want to hear that her walking wasn't enough to keep her muscles and bones strong. She didn't care that not staying strong put her at increased risk for injury. She just knew she might get hurt doing the lifts, so she quit on the spot. At the other extreme have been assorted clients who smile (behind gritted teeth?) and declare everything is just fine—until they report they were in pain for two days or aggravated a previous, unmentioned injury.

The approach of watching closely together with asking questions and really listening to answers has worked well for me, and I suspect that it will work well for you. It's likely that you will have a number of clients who have had not-so-great experiences with trainers. Clients' complaints about trainers in other gyms or different modalities tend to fall into two categories: "they injured me" or "I wasn't getting anything out of it." I suspect that both categories of complaints result from trainers or coaches who lack experience in working with people over, say, age 40. They may not understand that older clients do take longer to recover and may start at a lower level of strength and fitness—but (barring pathology) are capable of adding quite a lot of strength, given time, encouragement, adequate resistance, and adequate nutrition.

Individual differences

Just because someone can barely squat a broomstick doesn't mean she can't bench press a lot—and vice versa. The range of strength from one lift to the next may be remarkable, as is the range between superficially similar people.

Add weight

Once you are satisfied that your clients are performing the lifts in a safe and effective way, start adding weight. Most clients will reach that state quickly with RDL, bench press, and bent-over row, and a little slower with squats and push press, despite the significantly greater strength potential in the squats. And with power clean, learning technique takes quite a while for most people, although power clean has some particular weight considerations.

Take your time

Don't rush adding weight. Remember, especially for clients who arrived with fairly low strength, that their ability to add significant weight (and strength) on any of the lifts depends on their developing strong backs and abdominal muscles to stabilize their trunks. If you work the legs faster than the back can keep up, you are going to have sore backs or worse to contend with.

There's no one right way to proceed except by using your good judgment based on watching your clients and talking with them. Generally, younger clients can progress faster than older clients. Typically, when you think they're ready to handle more weight, add it in about 2.5 kg increments, less if the client is particularly slow to gain strength, which is truer for clients over 70 years or so.

Sometimes more is more

I make one exception to the "safe and effective" technique before adding weight, and that's for the power clean. I still try to make sure the amount of weight is safe and not what I would call heavy, but some clients seem to have a hard time lifting effectively with the power clean at low weights. They just can't seem to resist doing it all with their arms. For them, I add weight a little sooner so that they can feel if the bar is coming away from their body (among other power clean flaws) or they can feel the need to use their legs.

Testing

Once clients have plateaued in terms of weight increases on most lifts (they probably won't on all of them), we have a "testing" week. Most clients seem to plateau sooner on upper body lifts than with the lower body lifts, but that's OK. Pushing too fast on adding strength runs the risk of irritating connective tissue, which doesn't advance as quickly as muscle.

Testing consists of pushing your clients' limits a little and using their results to calculate a theoretical 1RM. You may want to give your clients a recovery week during the week before testing. (I do.) Here's how to proceed:

1. Recovery week. Two sets of 10 for each lift, with the top weight a couple of steps lighter than they have been doing.

2. Day 1 of test week.

   a. On clean, squat, and bench: Have lifter do 3 sets of 10 on 3 lifts (clean, squat, bench), with the last set for each lift being heavier than the client has done before. Ask clients to do up to 10 repetitions, stopping only if they are certain they cannot complete one more rep. Take note of how many repetitions they complete. (I generally don't ask lifters to complete more than 10 reps on this initial test, but another option is just to ask them to do as many reps as they can and record that number.)

   b. On push press, RDL, and rows: Repeat the 2 sets of 10 performed during recovery week.

3. Day 2 of test week. Reverse the workouts from day 1. That is, light on clean, squat, and bench, and heavy (testing) on push press, RDL, and bent-over row.

4. Calculate 1RM using this formula: Wt / (1.0278 - 0.0278 x reps) = 1RM. So, if someone lifted 30 kg for 10 reps, the formula would work like so: 30 / (1.0278 - 0.0278x10) = 30 / (1.0278 - 0.278) = 30 / 0.7498 = 40.01

As a practical matter, you probably aren't going to be whipping out a calculator to compute 1RMs. You can find apps to do so on your smartphone or tablet, or you can use the table I use. See Appendix A for 1RM table links. The apps I have seen have more bells and whistles than I want to fool with, and I find referencing a sheet of paper to be faster.

Test anxiety

It's funny what people worry about. It turns out that test anxiety occurs in the weight room. Remind clients that they can't fail the test, that it's just a way to see how they are doing and how to proceed. Alternatively, don't call it a test, call it an assessment.

WORKOUTS FOR ESTABLISHED LIFTERS

Once you have established 1RMs for your lifters, you can start working them through periodized workouts. A general scheme that works well is to have four-week cycles, with a testing-level workout during the 16th week, the end of the fourth cycle. Following are sample 16-week-session workouts. If your session starts after a break of some kind, you may want to add a day or week of lighter workouts to ease your

SAMPLE PROGRAM 1

week	reps	sets	%
1	5	3	65
2	5	4, 3*	75
3	5	2	65
4	5	3	80
5	4	4	75
6	4	4, 3*	85
7	4	3	70
8	4	3	90/70**
9	8	3	60
10	8	4	70
11	8	2	60
12	8	3	75/55**
13	6	3	65
14	6	3	75
15	6	2	60
16	6	3	88/60**

*On day 1, perform 4 sets of the cleans, squats, and bench presses, with both the 3rd and 4th sets at the maximum percentage shown. Perform 3 sets on the other three lifts. On day 2, reverse that pattern, with 4 sets on push press, RDL, and bent-over rows, and 3 sets on the others.

**On day 1, perform cleans, squats, and bench presses to the heavier percentage shown, and perform the other three lifts to the lower percentages. Reverse that pattern on day 2. Note: on the heavy lifts, distribute the work by about 10 percentage points, such that, for instance on week 8, the heavy lift sets would be performed at 70%, 80%, and 90%.

SAMPLE PROGRAM 2

week	reps	sets	%
1	10	3	55
2	10	3	65
3	10	2	50
4	10	3	70/55**
5	8	3	60
6	8	3	70
7	8	2	60
8	8	3	75/55**
9	6	3	65
10	6	3	75
11	6	2	60
12	6	3	85/65
13	5	3	70
14	5	3,4*	80
15	5	2	60
16	5	3	90/60**

*On day 1, perform 4 sets of the cleans, squats, and bench presses, with both the 3rd and 4th sets at the maximum percentage shown. Perform 3 sets on the other three lifts. On day 2, reverse that pattern, with 4 sets on push press, RDL, and bent-over rows, and 3 sets on the others.

**On day 1, perform cleans, squats, and bench presses to the heavier percentage shown, and perform the other three lifts to the lower percentages. Reverse that pattern on day 2. Note: on the heavy lifts, distribute the work by about 10 percentage points, such that, for instance on week 8, the heavy lift sets would be performed at 70%, 80%, and 90%.

lifters back into training. Countless books and articles have been written about various periodization schemes. If you have an approach you prefer, go with it.

The percentages shown in the tables are the maximum weight, to be lifted in the final set. (My classes work up to the maximum.)

LIFE CAN INTERFERE

As you can see, the general idea for presenting continually varied challenges is that the volume (the number of repetitions) and intensity (the amount of weight) vary from cycle to cycle. Each sample session program provides that the last cycle is the most challenging, and the last week of the session provides for testing.

The realities of life, however, mean that this arrangement is a prototype that you can use as the basis for your eventual workout plans, but holidays and vacations (yours!) probably will mean that you won't be able to adhere precisely to a 16-week rotation. In Chapter 8, you will find more information and suggestions for adapting the program to various types of interruptions.

It's helpful to remember that strength training in many gyms aims to improve athletic performance. Your clients, in contrast, generally are lifting to improve their daily lives. Hence, most won't have a Big Event that they are building toward. (If they do, you may want to draw on your additional knowledge of athletic training to create their program.) Instead, the aim of this program is to vary the ways clients use these fundamental lifts to stress the musculoskeletal system. As long as your lifters challenge their bodies and allow them to recover before the next challenge, they will get stronger—or, for those who are at their peak strength, they will lose strength more slowly than they otherwise might.

Best weightlifting training practices for non-competing adults, especially for anyone over, say, age 40, haven't been widely researched. Consequently, the workouts that my clients do (and that I do) are the result of experience and a little art as much as they are of science. Give them a try, review your results in the context of your specific clients, and adjust as appropriate.

CHAPTER 5

FACILITY NEEDS

To conduct your business, you are going to need a place for your clients to work out plus equipment for them to use. Options for your workout space include existing gyms, a building you own, or renting space. For most people, renting a space or fitting into an existing gym are most likely.

Regardless of where you land, the place must meet certain requirements, and most of this chapter focuses on your needs when looking to rent a space, but it also touches on fitting into an existing gym. Chapter 6 covers equipment.

FLOOR SPACE

There's a bit of a chicken-and-egg issue when it comes to determining how much floor space you are going to need for your weight room. That is, will you find your space and then decide how many and what size platform to use—or will you decide on the number and size of platforms, and then find a space that will accommodate them?

If you aren't particular about money or location, then go ahead and make your platform decisions first and then find your ideal space. If money and location (or both) are concerns, you may want to see what kind of space options are available before you invest in platforms.

That said, you will need space for three platforms. Standard platforms are 8 feet by 8 feet square, but 8 feet by 6 feet is workable. (More on that in the equipment chapter.) Eleiko, the noted Swedish barbell manufacturer, recommends at least 0.5 meter (about 20 inches) between platforms. In addition to the platforms, you need to allow room for a power rack or half rack abutting each platform. Rack footprints vary quite a bit, but you should allow at least 3 feet by 4 feet for each rack.

You also need to allow room for places to store various items and to conduct activities not directly related to lifting. Among the items you need to provide space for:

Reception. I use this term to refer to an area where you and/or your clients will keep their lifting records, pens and pencils, and so on. It doesn't necessarily have to be by the front door.

Desk. If you intend to do your management work in the workout space you seek to rent (as opposed to a home office), you need to allow room for a desk, computer, and so on. This could be part of the reception area or a separate, more private area.

Coat rack or hooks. Even if you live someplace that lacks cold weather, you still need to have a spot where people can store their hats, purses, and other personal items.

Changing room. I suppose a changing room isn't absolutely essential, but I highly recommend it. Some clients, at least some of the time, will arrive after (or before) work or attendance at some business or social function. They will appreciate being able to have a clean and at least somewhat private changing area. It is helpful to have enough room for a bench or chair, shelves where clients can stash their gym bag or street shoes, and hooks for hanging clothes. My changing room is about 8 feet square, and it seems to be a good size. It includes a coat-tree, a chair, and some shelves about 18 inches deep, deeper than probably necessary, but they nicely accommodate gym bags and so forth.

Dumbbell rack. Figure at least 2 feet deep by 3 feet wide for the rack plus 2 feet to 3 feet in front of the rack where a person would stand to get a dumbbell. Many dumbbell racks are longer than 3 feet.

Plate rack(s) if not part of power/half racks. These come in various sizes and shapes. Initially, you can simply store plates on the floor next to your power racks.

Restroom. If the space you are considering does not have its own restroom, make sure one is readily available. People will use it. (The space I started in had a restroom accessed by going outside and to the back of the building, and it was dreadful. People still used it.)

Supplies. Perhaps you won't have a separate supply room, but it's highly convenient to have a closet or out-of-the-way area to store paper supplies, cleaning supplies, and so forth.

OTHER PHYSICAL REQUIREMENTS

In addition to floor space, you need to consider the kind of floor—and ceiling—in your space.

The **floor** needs to be level and solid. Generally, that's going to mean concrete. The platforms will provide some cushioning for your joints, but you don't want to have the floor flexing when lifters jump or drop weights (which clients will rarely do, unless you teach the competition lifts). Besides, your space needs to be on the ground floor unless you have very unusual neighbors. Nobody wants a weight room overhead! (A client told me about someone he knows who lived above a weight room; that guy moved as soon as his lease was up.) It's OK if the floor has basic, short level-loop carpet. Carpet may reduce noise a touch, but it also can retain moisture. My current space has carpet under the platforms, and it hasn't been a problem.

The **ceiling**, meanwhile, needs to be high enough to allow overhead lifts by a reasonably tall person with long arms. A ceiling 9 feet high or more is desirable. (An 8-foot-6 ceiling might work if you turn away tall clients or ban bumper plates for overhead lifts.) Occasionally, you may have a high enough ceiling but light fixtures, heating-and-cooling ductwork, or other items hanging from the ceiling may interfere with overhead reach. Such a space might work, if you can arrange your platforms so that the ceiling-mounted items don't obstruct the lifts.

You may also want to consider the acoustic situation. Your lifters will generate noise, so if you will have nearby neighbors who can't tolerate noise—from the clanking of weights to potentially high-volume conversation—you could find yourself at odds with the neighbors, and that's to no one's benefit. (My next-door neighbor is a hair salon, and Marty, the proprietor, laughs at how many of his clients, upon hearing the hum of conversation and the clatter of weight plates, asks if there's a restaurant next door.) Another acoustic aspect is the resonance of the space. If your prospective space lacks sound-deadening surfaces, you can expect a significant din from plates clattering together as they slide onto bars and from the conversations sure to arise among clients.

Even if your space lacks sound-deadening qualities, there's no need to make the situation worse by planning to line the walls with mirrors. Mirrors seem de rigueur in many gyms. They aren't necessary and, arguably, may be counterproductive. You want your clients to be tuned in to what their bodies feel like, not what they look like. A side view is best for reviewing most lifts, and you just can't do that with mirrors—unless you turn your head, which would mess up the lift! (If a client needs to see what his lift looks like, take a video.)

HEATING AND COOLING

Unless you happen to live in, say, Santa Barbara, California, you are going to want a space that provides adequate heating or air-conditioning or both. It's both where I live. No doubt some people love working out without benefit of climate control, but, trust me, most people don't. As a general rule, you will want your space on the cool side, as lifting generates lots of internal heat. Air-conditioning provides the added comfort of reducing humidity.

If you find a space that is good except for the climate-control aspect, you may be able to adapt the space by retrofitting with an in-wall heating-and-cooling package unit, such as you may have seen in hotel rooms, or a "mini split," a ductless heating-and-cooling unit. Just make sure you get a system that is big enough to handle the demands of your space and climate.

LIGHTING

This program requires nothing special in the way of lighting. People just need to be able to see where they are going and to be able to read their workout records. I love natural light and appreciate having a space with big windows. However, windows have the drawback that people can see in as well as out. So, if your potential space has windows facing a street or sidewalk, you might wind up with shades or blinds closed much of the time, as your clients probably prefer not to be on view to passersby. Also, windows may present some complications to arranging your equipment and maintaining a steady temperature.

BEFORE YOU DECIDE

If you have found what you think is a good space at a price that works with your budget, do take a final review to make sure your space and equipment will work as you expect. Specifically, I recommend making a floor plan and try arranging your big items (the platforms and racks) on the plan. Cutting bits of paper to scale for your big items and moving them around on the plan is a handy way to do so. This step will help you to identify potential problems.

Doors, posts, and traffic paths are key potential challenges that can throw off your layout. Make sure you and your clients will be able to walk in and through the space. If you can afford it, more space beats less—usually. Still, people can fit three platforms and plate storage in a generous two-car garage, although overhead space can be tricky. My studio has plenty of floor space, but a door, a post, and a gentle slope to part of the floor (which I didn't notice until actually placing the equipment) resulted in an arrangement that works, but is not exactly as I would have chosen. I wound up rotating one platform so that the slope is front-to-back on the platform, rather than side to side. This change works pretty well for the lifting, but it means that I must move around to make sure I get a good look at each lifter.

LEASE TERMS

The hope and expectation is that your business will take off, but it's hard to know until you are using the space whether it is exactly what you need. If it isn't, you may want to move. As a result, it makes sense to avoid a long-term lease until you know whether it's a place you want to stay. Be sure to read the lease terms carefully or consult an attorney to review it. Also, depending on your local market, you may be able to negotiate terms that suit your needs better than what the property owner or her agent initially proposes. Besides prices, dates, and so forth, you also can request actions you want the property owner to take before you move in.

EXISTING GYM

If you can't find a suitable space or want to start on a smaller scale, starting at an existing gym can be a good way to build your business at minimal cost. If you know of a gym whose space and equipment fit your needs, create a proposal spelling out what you are going to do, what you are willing to pay, and what you need from the gym. Then approach the manager with that proposal. Your ability to get satisfying terms will depend on many factors, not least of which is whether you can boost the gym's bottom line, but if the existing-gym approach makes most sense to you, then there's no harm in asking. A proposal that brings people in during non-peak hours is likely to get the warmest reception.

AT YOUR HOME

Except in highly urbanized areas where people primarily travel on foot or by public transportation, your business will generate automobile traffic. That means you may not be able to operate out of your home unless you live in a rural area (and sometimes even then) due to various local ordinances regarding home businesses or because you don't want to annoy your neighbors. If you are close enough to a population center but don't have zoning restrictions, then it is possible for you to operate out of your home, as my first coach demonstrated in his garage. If so, you still will need to consider the physical requirements as described herein as well as parking.

LOCATION, LOCATION

Although some clients will travel distances to take advantage of your program, most people like places close to where they live or work—or en route between two places they frequent. If you are renting (or buying), chances are the most convenient location may not offer the best price. Aim for someplace that clients can easily get to but that is sufficiently inexpensive that the rent doesn't drain your bank account. The real estate environment is always evolving, so keep looking even if you don't find what you want right away. Ask everyone you know for suggestions, and you may be pleased at what you find.

THE UNEXPECTED

Your business will be unique to you and your locale, so remember this chapter provides general information. You may have added needs with regard to, say, parking. Try to visualize how you and your clients, individually and together, will experience the space. Then do your best. It's a process! And moving is always an option, even if it is a pain in the neck.

CHAPTER 6

EQUIPMENT AND SUPPLIES

Even though we are talking relatively small classes, you still will need at least a modest amount of bars and weights to accommodate your clientele. In addition, you will need some more generic supplies. Here is a list of the lifting equipment needs. Following it is a list of general supplies and equipment. The rest of the chapter will detail these items.

Piecemeal is OK

It's great to have all of the equipment, but you don't have to get everything all at once, and some things are entirely optional. Start with what you need right away, and add as you go along.

- Olympic barbells
- Olympic weight plates
- Lighter-weight bars or barbells and plates
- Lifting platforms
- Blocks for barbell support
- Power racks
- Weight bench
- Other weights: dumbbells, ankle weights, medicine balls
- Miscellaneous supplies

It's easy to focus on the above key equipment, but don't forget the smaller items that will make things run smoothly.

- Coat hooks
- Seating
- Wall clock
- Wall calendar
- Bulletin board
- Multi-tray storage for records
- Pens and pencils
- Clipboards
- Cleaning supplies
- Hygiene and first-aid supplies
- Changing room furnishings

LIFTING EQUIPMENT

First a note about units of weight. I chose to buy barbells and plates scaled in kilograms. I was accustomed to using kilograms. Competitions are conducted in kilograms. Kilograms are cool. And it turns out that kilograms have an added advantage for new lifters more familiar with imperial pounds: these novices don't obsess over how much weight they're lifting because it sounds light! The downside to using kilogram-scaled equipment is that it can be harder to find, especially if you are hoping to score some used equipment.

That said, I will be talking mostly in kilograms, but where specific weights are mentioned, I'll list both metric and imperial measures.

It's all good

Don't sweat the decision about pounds versus kilograms. Just pick one and stick with it.

Olympic barbells

You need at least six Olympic barbells. You may want 15 kg (33 lb.) barbells, 20 kg (44 lb.) barbells or a combination. (I have four 15 kg and two 20 kg.)

Your barbells are crucial to your lifting program, so this is one area where you should take the trouble and expense of buying decent bars. You might be able to buy used barbells, but be choosy. I bought used plates almost exclusively but I splurged on new bars and don't regret it—especially after I picked up a couple of used bars that turned out to be of poor quality.

The long Olympic bar is 20 kg, and the shorter one is 15 kg. The chrome bar with threaded collars is a 7 kg (15 lb.) standard bar.

Online, you can find many guides to choosing and buying barbells. One such guide can be found at http://garagegymbuilder.com. Appendix A lists more. Availability of decent bars has improved since I started my business, a fact I assume is related to the growth in popularity of CrossFit gyms, so that may help you.

If you haven't done much Olympic lifting, you may think a bar is a bar, but you are mistaken. Olympic bars are more flexible than powerlifting bars, a good trait when you are executing the quick movements of Olympic lifts. They also need to have better spin than powerlifting or general-purpose bars. Good bars also feel better in your hands.

Case in point: When I started buying equipment, I picked up three secondhand bars for little money, mostly as add-ons when I bought used plates from individuals. I wound up not using any of those bars. I got rid of two and have the third stashed in a corner. Two of them were uncomfortably stiff when trying to do Olympic lifts. The third (and remaining) bar is stiff, has rough knurling, and the shaft is fatter than is standard.

For our program, you won't need to buy $1,000 competition bars, but you need ones that have the following characteristics. Prices most likely will be $300–$500, give or take:

Which size. My clientele is 90% female, hence my decision to buy more 15 kg (33 lb.) bars than 20 kg (44 lb.) bars. Besides weighing less, the other important thing about the 15 kg bars is that the grip is smaller than that of 20 kg bars, at 25 mm versus 28 mm (0.98 inch versus 1.1 inch) in diameter. The difference in grip sounds insignificant, but you definitely can feel the difference once accustomed to one over the other, and the smaller grip tends to work better for smaller hands. In fact, the grip size is more important than the bar weight, because you can always add more plates to make for a heavier lift!

Good spin. The sleeve should rotate smoothly and freely. That's because when a bar turns (relative to the ground) during a lift, you don't want the plates to turn with it. A stiff or sticky sleeve means turning the bar will be very difficult when loaded. Bar aficionados may demand needle bearings instead of the more common and less expensive bushings, but for our purposes bushings should be fine.

Decent flex. If you've ever watched competitive weightlifting, you have seen the bar bow downward on the ends when a lifter brings the bar to her shoulders in a clean, and then the bar springs back to straight. If the lifter has her technique down, she will use the bar's spring, or whip, to boost the bar overhead for the jerk. Now, your clients aren't likely to be throwing around the kind of weight that those Olympians are lifting, but having a little whip nevertheless is helpful. I didn't think so until I tried a power clean with a powerlifting bar. That stiff bar made the lift significantly harder.

Comfortable knurling. Knurling is the roughened or scored area where a lifter places her hands. The knurling needs to be pronounced enough that a person can get a good grip, but not so rough as to be painful.

Buyer beware

Some sellers will call any bar with a 50 mm / 2-inch sleeve an Olympic bar. It's true that these bars should accept the weight plates used for Olympic lifting, but they may be power bars or some other stiffer bar or a bar with poor spin.

Olympic weight plates

Minimum 12 plates (6 pairs) with 150 mm (2-inch) holes in each of the following sizes:

- 🏋 1.25 kg (2.75 lb.) per plate
- 🏋 2.5 kg (5.5 lb.)
- 🏋 5 kg (11 lb.)
- 🏋 10 kg (22 lb.)

Optional additional plates, one or more pairs of each of the following sizes:

- 🏋 15 kg (33 lb.) per plate
- 🏋 20 kg (44 lb.)
- 🏋 "Fractional" plates

The 1.25 kg, 2.5 kg, and 5 kg plates most likely will be cast iron or steel. The heavier plates may be iron or steel, or they can be true Olympic plates known as bumper plates, for their ability to withstand (and cushion) the impact when loaded bars are dropped from overhead. Bumper plates are dense rubber with a standard diameter of 450 mm (18 inches), whereas the lighter plates' diameter varies with the weight. The smallest standard Olympic bumper plates weigh 10 kg (22 lb.), although you may be able to find 10-pound (4.5 kg) bumpers.

You can remove rust

If you buy used iron or steel plates, some of them likely will look pretty rusty. You can find a wide array of potential rust-removing techniques online, or you can use the method I used, which my friend (and letterpress hobbyist) Neil recommended. It's easy, inexpensive, and does a good job—or at least a good enough job if you don't require perfect:

Fill a plastic tub or bucket with basic white vinegar, available by the gallon at the grocery store. Place rusty plates in the vinegar and soak over-night. Try to make sure the vinegar can access all surfaces. The next day, wearing nitrile or rubber gloves, scrub plates with a fairly stiff scrub brush, rinse well, and let dry. Voila! Clean plates. If they're still too rusty for your taste, just soak longer.

A couple of additional notes: Some people recommend a follow-up soak of 10 minutes or so in a mixture of 1 cup baking soda (sodium bicarbonate) and water to neutralize any remaining acid. I didn't take this step, and it hasn't been a problem. Adding 1 cup salt to 1 gallon vinegar is supposed to increase the acidity and therefore the rust-removal potential.

Paint helpful

Follow rust removal with a combination primer-top coat in different colors on the 2.5 kg and 5 kg plates, and give unpainted plates a coat of paste wax to protect them from further rust. The paint will make bar loading easier, as you and your clients will be able to distinguish at a glance how much weight is on the bar. It's probably best to use the color scheme specified by the International Weightlifting Federation (see Appendix A), but I went with colors readily available at the hardware store. It hasn't been a problem, but potentially could confuse experienced weightlifters or deter future buyers should you decide to sell your equipment.

Although your clients will be doing some Olympic moves, they rarely (if ever) will need bumper plates, which is handy because bumpers generally are significantly more expensive than metal plates and they rarely seem to be available to buy used. Having some bumper plates available (I have one pair each of 10 kg and 15 kg bumpers) is nice as it allows the option of dropping bars—and clients seem to enjoy using them as they feel lighter than they look. They also make good, sturdy bases for step-ups. But you will be fine with metal plates, especially to start.

Whether you acquire the plates I list as optional may depend on your clients' strength, your (or your clients') tolerance for mathematical rounding, and cash flow. But here is why you may or may not want to buy them:

15 kg plates. It's likely that some of your clients at some stage will find 15 kg plates useful. Even if some of your early clients have enough experience and strength for 15 kg plates, they most likely will be able to put enough weight on their bar without them. If you find you are running low on plates, then you can go buy them! I have two pair metal and one pair bumper plates at 15 kg, and they do get used.

20 kg plates. I have two pairs of (metal) 20 kg plates but we never use them. They're heavy (surprise!), and most people would rather load up a couple of 10 kg plates or a 15 kg and 5 kg plate than to wrestle a 20 kg plate on and off a bar. Of course, if you aim for younger and stronger clients, you may find these useful.

Fractional plates. These are small plates with small increments so that you can load a bar to the nearest kilogram. You can buy fractional plates in sets (typically, one pair each of 0.5 kg, 1 kg, 1.5 kg, and 2 kg). Some sets are available with the smallest increment at 0.25 kg. Fractional plates are where your and your clients' tolerance for approximations comes into play. The time will come when workouts will be based on a percentage of their estimated 1-repetition maximum, so calculations may tell them they need to lift 18.9 kg (for instance). Should they lift 17.5 kg or 20 kg, the weights they can attain through the recommended plate purchases? What a dilemma! If you or your clients can't bear to make that kind of judgment call, you may want fractional plates. For quite a while I had 0.5 kg and 1 kg plates, allowing clients to load the bar to, say, 21 kg or 23.5 kg. They were so in demand that a client, impatient (I guess) that I wasn't buying more of them, bought and donated a set with little Lifesaver-looking plates weighing 0.25 kg, 0.5 kg, 0.75 kg, and 1 kg. That seems to me to be more trouble in the bar-loading department than I want to fool with, but at least some of my clients love them.

Lighter-weight bars or barbells and plates

Chances are better than good that your beginning lifters will need to start by practicing with bars that weigh less than 15 kg. Following is the inventory of bars I keep at my studio. This selection allows lifters to start light and gradually increase their loads in approximately 2 kg increments:

- 2 kg (4.4 lb.)
- 3 kg (6.6 lb.)
- about 7 kg (15 lb.) with enough plates to go up to about 13 kg

The 2 kg and 3 kg bars are 5-foot lengths of 3/4-inch (inside diameter) PVC filled with sand (the 2 kg) or filled with a 5-foot piece of No. 5 (5/8-inch) rebar plus sand to eliminate movement of rebar. These do not get significant amounts of use, but they are good to have for new lifters. Sometimes we augment the 3 kg bar with a pair of 1-pound or 2.5-pound wrist weights to provide a graded increase when someone isn't quite ready for a 7 kg bar. It isn't elegant, but it gets the job done, and people don't stay at such light weights for long.

What I call 7 kg bars are "standard" weightlifting bars with a grip of about 1 inch and ends that accommodate plates with 1-inch (approximate) holes. Such bars are sold as 15-pound bars, are inexpensive (about $30 new) and widely available at sporting goods stores, discount stores, garage sales, and online. They're worth as much or less than you pay for them. I hate these bars, but for most lifters they are used only temporarily, so I tolerate them. Here's what I don't like about them: the collars are a pain to use; the knurling is rough; the chrome may flake off and poke somebody's fingers; and, worst of all, the plates may hang up on the bar's threaded ends when you do a power clean, adding an awkward degree of difficulty to the lift. One of these days, I may spring for a couple of decent 10 kg "junior" Olympic bars, but until then, my new lifters who lack much strength use these. (I console myself by noting that the new lifters are more tolerant of these bars than I am—and by the hope that they'll be motivated to move up to the Olympic bars.)

You also will need a stock of plates for the standard bars. I have never seen plates for standard bars that are gauged in kilograms, so I have about a dozen 2.5-pound plates (1.1 kg) and a half dozen 5-pound (2.3 kg) plates. So as to reduce the confusion of switching back and forth between pounds and kilograms, I have marked up the standard plates with kilogram equivalents and in practice think of the small plates as 1 kg plates and the large ones as 2 kg plates. We aren't using them to set world records (or to balance a scale selling gold), so these small increments don't matter.

Lifting platforms

The lifting platforms serve as workout stations. The platforms provide a bit of cushion for lifters' joints as well as a somewhat resilient surface for the rare occasions (for our purposes) when people need to drop their weights. Typical full-size gym platforms are 8 feet square and 1 1/2-inches to 2-inches thick.

You can buy nicely finished weightlifting platforms from various suppliers, and reduced-cost platform packages are also available. Or you can do it yourself and save money. Appendix A lists online articles about how to build such a platform.

Your lifters are unlikely to need platforms quite as substantial as the $1,000 models you can buy or even the less-expensive ones you can build. My studio uses stall mats (intended for use in stalls for horses) to make simple and serviceable 8-foot by 6-foot platforms. Each platform consists of two 6-foot by 4-foot by 3/4-inch rubber mats to form the platform alongside half racks. If you live anywhere near a horse or farm supply store (Tractor Supply Co. stores are a good nation-wide source), you can buy these mats for a very reasonable price, about $30 per mat in 2018. Important notes if you decide to go this direction:

Each mat weighs almost 100 pounds, so plan accordingly for picking them up at the store and moving them into your space. Moving them is at least a two-person job because they are as unwieldy as they are heavy, or you can try a product called EZGrip Mat Mover, usually available at stores that sell the mats. (See Appendix A.) I have no experience with it, but the item is designed specifically for moving stall mats and has great online reviews.

Expect the mats to smell like a tire store. With time and ventilation the rubber smell goes away. Tractor Supply estimates two to four weeks, but expect it to take longer.

You probably will want a frame. Mats will migrate on a concrete floor unless they go wall to wall. Heavy as they are, mats are remarkably mobile when laid on concrete without anything to impede their movement. You can buy metal platform frames through some sporting goods suppliers. I had a carpenter make wood frames to hold the mats in place for me. I have also seen use of a polyure-thane adhesive caulk recommended, but I have no experience in using it. I do know that double-sided tape or non-skid carpet tape seem inadequate to the job.

They could stain floors. If you want to place mats over wood or carpet, be advised that the natural oils in the rubber could cause discoloration.

They can be cut. If you want an 8-foot-square platform, you can place two mats side-by-side to make an 8-foot by 6-foot platform, and then use a carpet knife to cut 2-foot-wide pieces to add to the 6-foot edge.

Blocks for barbell support

In this program, your clients will be performing power cleans, but few will be strong enough to do so with ordinary bumper plates, at least not at first. The answer: blocks.

You can buy very nice, expensive, and heavy-duty blocks designed for heavy-duty practice doing pulls or jerks. That's going to be overkill for our purposes, because we aren't going to be dropping heavily loaded bars on them. All we need is a solid unit that will hold a loaded bar at approximately 215 mm (8.5 inches) above the ground. (If you are doing the math, that's a little below the middle of a 450 mm plate to allow for the diameter of the bar.) I haven't found anything built for this purpose, but you can improvise any number of ways, such as with a pair of nice, solid step stools. I suspect that some heavy-duty industrial crates might work. But here are two ways that are sure to work:

Build wood blocks. If you have (or know someone who has) basic carpentry skills, you can build your own. My coach's were pretty rough-looking, but they did the job. A friend designed and built my very nicely finished ones, as shown in the accompanying photographs.

The wood block for supporting a barbell without bumper plates for power cleans is about 8.25 inches high. The base is 14 inches long, and the stacked lumber portion is about 12 inches long. The bevel on the top two pieces makes a convenient hand-hold for moving the blocks.

Staples and inset screws securely fasten the block pieces without projections.

Putting smooth, rounded edges on the blocks is thoughtful for your clients, as that step reduces splinters, and the inverted, beveled bits on top makes it easy to pick up and move the blocks. (Note: dimensional lumber that is nominally 2 inches thick actually is 1.5 inches, and 1-inch nominal wood is actually 0.75 inches thick.)

- Bottom: 2-by-6

- Stack: 4 pieces 2-by-4

- Top: 1 piece 1-by-4

- Stops: 3-inch by 1-inch (give or take) pieces of plywood or molding, such as half-round, quarter-round, or base shoe.

The parts need to be solidly attached to one another but without screws or other fasteners poking out. They won't be receiving dropped bars (or at least not much), but they will take some abuse. Finish with a couple of coats of polyurethane, to help reduce splintering that may occur at the edges over time.

Stack up pieces of stall mat. Stall mats (as described above in the platforms discussion) can be cut into pieces approximately 1-foot square and stacked. Eleven should give you about the right height, and you can get 24 from one 4-by-6-foot mat. Hence 1 mat = 1 pair of blocks with a little to spare. These would be less movable than the wood blocks described above and considerably heavier.

To cut mats, mark your lines, then use a metal straight edge to score the mats deeply with a carpet knife or utility knife. You can then bend or fold the mat away from the initial cut, and finish cutting completely through the mat. If the stacked pieces migrate, you can use a non-petroleum-based adhesive to glue them together. You can ask at a hardware store for adhesives to bond natural rubber.

Power racks

You will need three power racks of one kind or another. The general options are a full power rack, a half rack, and squat rack. They hold a barbell to aid in lifts and generally are made of steel. Key considerations are that they are sturdy, stable, and allow for easy adjustment of the bar height. This is another area where cheap is a bad idea, although you probably don't need gear for professional football players, either.

Full power rack. Safest are top-of-the-line racks/cages that are large enough for a lifter to stand inside while squatting or doing overhead presses or to position a bench inside for bench-pressing. Such a power rack will have side arms or bars to keep the barbell from landing on you or pushing you far forward or backward should you fail in any of those lifts. It also will have adjustable supports for holding the barbell between lifts.

> **Pros:** Durable (unless you buy a cheaply made one), safest option, versatile, can hold large amounts of weight, probably provides pull-up bar (if you care).
>
> **Cons:** Takes up most floor space, most expensive, may be inconvenient for swapping bars.
>
> **Notes:** Be sure to get one tall enough, such as 90 inches, to accommodate tall people with long arms doing overhead lifts. Racks may have option of pegs to store weight plates on the sides.

Half rack. A so-called half rack doesn't permit the lifter inside the rack. Rather, pins or J-cups hold the barbell on the face of the uprights at variable heights. They may have projecting arms as a safety feature to stop the bar's descent during a failed lift.

> **Pros:** Durable, safe, may take up less floor space (or not), less expensive than full rack, doesn't have to be taller than tallest lifters' shoulders.

Cons: Probably not quite as sturdy as full rack, as uprights are closer together (from front to back of rack). Safety arms for stopping bar on a failed lift may be less reliable than on full rack because they can't stop lifter falling backward.

Notes: Rack may have option of pegs to store weight plates on sides.

Squat rack. Squat racks generally have a single upright support on each end of the barbell and thus tend to be less stable than full or half power racks. The uprights may be two separate pieces or be yoked together (which is more stable). Heavy-duty, tall squat racks with plenty of vertical adjustments and with a yoke or crossbar of some kind for stability may be plenty adequate for your needs.

Pros: Take less floor space, possibly less expensive.

Cons: Safety arms for stopping bar on a failed lift may be less reliable than on full rack because they can't stop lifter falling backward. May not provide enough height adjustment to be useful for Romanian deadlifts or bench presses.

Note: May have option of safety bars to catch missed lift.

Other options. Besides the above racks, you may want to consider these options, depending on your budget and space needs:

- Wall-mounted rack. Single pair of uprights with top that bolts to a wall.

- Custom-built rack. This is the option I took. A local metal fabricator constructed smallish half racks to my specifications, as my space required a small footprint. The cost was somewhat less than commercially constructed racks, and there were no freight costs.

Height adjustments

Make sure holes for barbell height adjustments are at most 2 inches apart.

Weight bench

This program includes bench presses, so you are going to need at least two benches. I recommend simple, flat benches, as they are sturdy and easy to move to and from the racks. Unless you have tons of room, you aren't likely to want a separate bench-rack combination. Adjustable benches aren't necessary for our purposes and are prone to pinching fingers when moved around. A third or even fourth bench isn't a bad idea, but space considerations may dictate fewer. Besides presses, you also may use a bench for dumbbell bent-over rows and some core work.

Watch for insubstantial bench

Try out your benches or buy commercial-grade benches, as there are some pretty flimsy benches out there that will not stand up to frequent, daily use.

Other weights: dumbbells, ankle weights, medicine balls

The "other weights" supplement the barbells and plates and provide means for you to adapt certain lifts to accommodate various physical limitations. They also can provide added intensity to some core work and allow you to increase weight in small increments. These are on the low-priority end of your weight equipment.

Dumbbells. Dumbbells are widely available secondhand, commonly for 50 cents to $1 a pound. (Apart from one online store, I have not seen dumbbells available in kilogram sizes.) Through Craigslist, I have accrued dumbbell pairs of 5, 8, 10, 12, 15, 20, 25, 30, 40, and 45 pounds. If you too acquire them bit by bit, start with the lighter ones and work up. A second option is to get a dumbbell bar on which you can load standard weight plates. That's how I fill the occasional need for a 35-pound dumbbell. The dumbbell bar is significantly less convenient than the dumbbells at fixed weights. Also available are selector-type dumbbell sets that essentially make quick and easy work of loading a dumbbell bar. These are fairly costly, but compared with a standard dumbbell bar they are easy to use and quiet. They also take up less room than a set of fixed-weight dumbbells.

Ankle weights. These can serve multiple purposes. Light wrist or ankle weights—such as 1-pound and 2.5-pounders—can be used on PVC bars to bridge the gap between a 3 kg and 7 kg bar. They also can be used on wrists to provide incremental increases between, say, 20- and 25-pound dumbbells. Last, they can provide added intensity for some core exercises.

Medicine balls. Probably the least important of these auxiliary weights, medicine balls can be used to add intensity to core exercises.

Miscellaneous exercise supplies

You may or may not want to provide the following items for your lifters:

- hand chalk (I don't provide).
- straps to aid grip for Romanian deadlift (I do provide).
- exercise mats (I do provide).

Make your own straps

Make simple and inexpensive lifting straps at home using 1-inch tubular webbing such as what rock climbers use or flat nylon webbing such as that used in slacklining—or dog leashes. You can buy it by the foot at outdoors stores, hardware stores, or online. Sew ends of an 18-inch length of webbing together for a loop-type strap. Another option: fold over about 1.5 inches on one end of that webbing and stitch in place to create a small slot, then pass opposite end of webbing through that slot to create a loop for wrists.

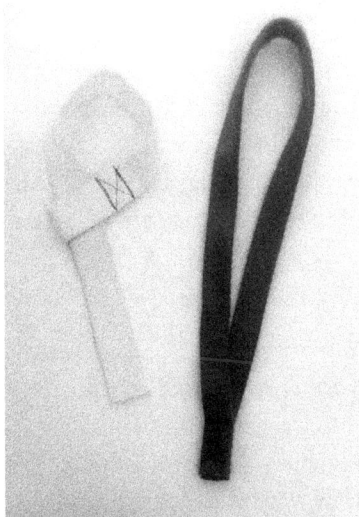

Two types of straps can be easily made from inexpensive nylon webbing.

SUPPLIES AND OTHER EQUIPMENT

It's easy to forget that your gym or studio requires more than heavy things to lift. This section discusses some of those other items, in no particular order. See Appendix A for some specific recommendations.

Coat hooks

People are going to need somewhere to hang their coats, handbags, and umbrellas. If you have to choose between sturdy and pretty, go for sturdy.

Chairs or bench

People—including you—may want or need to sit down from time to time. So get a few chairs. I managed to snag at a very low price a few heavy-duty but lightweight secondhand chairs from a party-rental place. If your business grows as we hope it will, you will be glad you have sturdy chairs that won't tip or break with regular use. A bench also would work for seating.

Timekeeping

Get a legible wall clock (with a second hand) and a wall calendar for both you and your clients. The clock will help you keep track of where you are in your day, and your clients can use it to keep track of how long they have been resting— or holding their planks. The calendar is helpful for reference when people want to tell you their vacation dates and for a visual reminder of holidays and such.

Bulletin board

You can put your wall calendar here if you like, but it's also nice to be able to post items on a bulletin board. The possibilities include health and weightlifting articles, news items featuring your business or your clients, and posters or bulletins of general interest. From time to time my clients have something that they want to post, such as flyers for fundraisers, and they seem to appreciate my permitting them to do so for a week or two.

Multi-tray storage for records

This item may be optional, depending on how you operate. I decided it was easier for me and for my clients to keep their weightlifting records at the studio, so each tray of this item holds the workout sheets or notebooks for one class. (See Chapter 8 for more on this subject.) Office supply stores may call them desk trays. Wall pockets also would work. I would recommend against stacking trays, as they tend to be unstable.

Other 'office' supplies

I provide pens and pencils as well as clipboards for clients to use to record their workouts. (Actually, I provide pencils, and the one or two pens I supplied starting more than six years ago have somehow multiplied to the excess quantity I have now.) Small wall hooks next to racks allow lifters to place their clipboards at eye level as they work out.

Staying sharp

Little things count. I provide good-quality wood pencils that I sharpen weekly, and clients tell me regularly how happy those sharp pencils make them. Who knew?

Cleaning and related supplies

Maybe you will hire a janitorial service, but if you are doing it yourself, remember that you will need such items as a vacuum cleaner, broom, and mop for floors plus cleaning products that suit your preferences. Also, you will need a trash bin or two and probably a recycling bin.

Hygiene and first-aid supplies

Unless provided by your landlord or outside vendor, you will need or want to provide all or most of the following:

- first-aid kit
- hand soap
- paper towels
- toilet paper

- disinfectant wipes
- hand sanitizer
- facial tissues

Presumably, the above items are self-explanatory. Perhaps of note regarding the first-aid kit, adhesive bandages for the occasional small cut and instant cold packs have been the most frequently used items from my kit.

Changing-room furnishings

Your needs may depend on your space, but you will find it helpful to provide a chair, a mirror, hooks or a coat-tree, and shelves (or possibly bigger or more widely spaced hooks) for people to park their gym bags or street shoes. I also provide facial wipes and facial tissues so that clients can do some minimal freshening up if they choose.

CHAPTER 7

GET CLIENTS

Space, equipment, program ... what more could you need? Oh, yeah. Clients. Here is where your personal network comes in, unless you love marketing as much as you love weightlifting. Me, I'd rather help people get strong than be in a constant state of sales.

In this chapter, you will read a little about what worked for me, suggestions for additional promotional opportunities, and some general marketing tips if the practice is entirely new to you. Entire books have been written about how to promote small businesses (links to a couple of book lists appear in Appendix A), so you should in no way consider this chapter to be exhaustive. What I hope you will take away from this chapter is the knowledge that you need to:

- keep in mind your primary target client.
- cite benefits of personal interest to your prospective client.
- remember "old tech" and use social media, too.

This chapter focuses on capturing new or first-time clients. Gaining renewals and expanding the business is discussed in Chapter 10.

YOUR TARGET CLIENT

When you are first starting, you may think, "I'll take anybody who will pay me!" And maybe you will. But you can't target the whole world, or at least you can't target everyone and have a high rate of success with your marketing efforts. Hence, the idea is to identify your preferred or most likely client, and present a message to capture the attention of that potential client.

Although this weightlifting program will work for people of almost any age, my target client (and my reason for writing this book) is a woman age 40 or older. As previously noted, I have clients ages 16 to 81, male and female, and I'm thrilled to have such a cross-generational clientele of all shapes and sizes, but I aim for people in their forties, fifties, and sixties. This is an age group (especially those over 50) that is beginning to see the effects of diminishing strength and, for some, diminishing bone density. Hence, these individuals realize that the value of getting and staying strong goes beyond the cosmetic.

This also is an age group that may not feel particularly at home in large gyms. Perhaps it's a bigger issue where I live—in a small city with a large university— but many clients mention to me their discomfort with the crowds, the preponderance of twenty-somethings in the local gyms, and the attendant focus on appearance. Older people want to look good, too, but most of them know that the implied promises of achieving some ideal, sculpted body just aren't realistic. They aren't trying to "get in shape" to go to the beach or fit into a party dress. They want to be strong to pursue the activities in life that give them satisfaction, whether it's working in the garden, playing with grandchildren, or being able to help their children move furniture.

As to the sex of clients, my emphasis has been on women. That's for multiple reasons. The primary one is that women as a group don't have a good understanding of what they need to do to get strong, and they don't seem to get much encouragement to do so. Still, many are reading the increasingly frequent, publicized advice that strength training is an important part of physical well-being, and they are interested in learning.

Some have tried other approaches with little success. A typical commercial gym points them to a few machines and sets them loose. Women who can afford a personal trainer get more instruction, but, again, much of it likely will be machine-focused. I also hear complaints about trainers who don't seem to be sufficiently conscious of dealing with a "mature" body. And many, if not most, women are intimidated or feel uncomfortable in the weight rooms of commercial gyms, which tend to be dominated by young men moving at least moderately big weights. Lots of men don't embrace that setting, either.

FINDING THE TARGET

So how do you reach your target client? Some of it, of course, may depend on details about your target, but you should take a multipronged approach if you can, with a heavy emphasis on your personal network. That was relatively easy for me, because my target client was largely my own demographic. Hence, I sought clients by email, handbills, and personal conversations as they arose with personal friends and acquaintances. Some of those friends and acquaintances also passed the information on to their networks, too.

The email message I sent (see the content in the next section of this book) went to all women in my contact list who I thought would be good candidates, primarily based on where they lived. The handbills were simple photocopies providing the same information as in the email, and I handed them to people I knew or met. The result is rather like social media but a bit more personal and probably more selective. I made no cold calls and didn't need to.

My goal was to get at least four clients per class for that first session, and I more than succeeded. By contacting dozens of local friends and acquaintances, I wound up with 19 students for those first three classes—seven more than my goal. For the summer session, I had 22 students and added a fourth class, and for the fall I had 25 clients. A year after starting the business, I had 33 clients in those four classes.

It felt good, and this growth occurred entirely due to word-of-mouth "publicity," without benefit of any paid advertising, without a Facebook page, without a Twitter feed, without an article or post by a local newspaper or blogger. I'm not saying those can't be useful, but I am saying they are not necessary. Targeting my own demographic made identifying potential clients easier and gave me credibility with them.

But what if your target client isn't your demographic? Again, use your network, but use it for getting leads, especially for your very first clients. By getting leads and referrals from your friends and acquaintances, you automatically have more credibility than you would by advertising or sending what might appear to be a spam email. If you are younger than your target audience, it wouldn't hurt to make clear your sensitivity to working with people with more, ahem, life experience.

Get the word out before you launch

You may be tempted to stay mum on your business plans until you are ready to launch, but try not to wait. Once you've decided to go for it, start talking about it to friends, relatives, acquaintances, coworkers. By doing so you are laying the groundwork for getting leads to your first clients.

This step may be trickier if you are working at a gym, plan to go out on your own, and don't want to tip off or irritate your current employer. That doesn't mean you need to keep a lid on your plans, but it does mean you'd be smart not to talk about it at your employer's gym or to clients there.

Ideally, you will talk about your planned business during your ramp-up period, as you are looking for space, equipment, and so on. That way, your friends won't be surprised when you ask them for leads to prospective clients. Asking in person or by phone is wonderful, albeit time-consuming. If your contacts use email, you can send a prospecting email like the one that follows or post a similar item to Facebook. Facebook is less personal (unless you do it via Facebook Messenger), but it's fast:

Hi, [name],

You know I love weightlifting, and I'm about to launch a new business teaching weightlifting for strength. I would be honored and thrilled if you would pass on the attached information to your friends, relatives, and acquaintances who are [describe target client] or otherwise interested in weightlifting. If you prefer, you could send me their contact information, and I'll contact them directly.

I'm very excited about this venture and sharing this very effective program for getting strong with people in a small-group setting! I'll keep you posted on how things progress.

Thanks for whatever help you can offer! Hope you are well.

Kind regards,

[Your name, telephone number, email address]

P.S. If you are interested, I'd love to have you give it a try, too!

Of course, there are endless added ways you can get exposure using the internet. If you are a child of the internet and think your prospective clients are, too, then go for it. There are thousands of books on internet marketing and on social media marketing that can help you along. See Appendix A for links.

Other easy ways to get leads

- Include a "signature" on all emails saying something on the order of:

  Alex Strong, owner of [business name], [phone], [email]

  Contact me now for session starting [date]

- Once you are in business, reward your current clients for bringing in new clients. (Current clients are your best advocates!) I let my clients know I give them a cash gift (or credit on fees) of $10 when someone they refer signs up.

WHAT TO TELL PROSPECTIVE CLIENTS

Remember again who is your target client. Everything you know about that person or persons points to the message of your marketing efforts. Selling benefits is the name of the game. So don't forget these benefits when talking to prospective clients (or people from whom you are seeking leads) whether in person, in print, or electronically:

- get stronger and more powerful
- gain flexibility
- exercise in a time-efficient manner
- improve coordination
- strengthen the core
- build stronger bones
- enjoy social interaction with classmates
- improve balance
- work out in a welcoming environment
- get personalized attention and instruction
- gain strength and improve body mechanics to make life activities easier

Weightlifting also provides benefits that aren't the primary reason for the activity but may be big bonuses for some clients. Having a clear idea of your target client (and your decisions about operations and facilities) will determine whether these are benefits to mention:

- likely improvement in pelvic floor tone (meaning elimination or significant reduction in stress incontinence)
- no wall of mirrors (if true for your space)
- no deafening music (if true for your space)
- likely improvement in athletic performance

Checklist for communications

- benefits
- request for action (that is, ask them to sign up and tell them how!)
- time, days, and location of classes
- your contact information
- your qualifications
- price
- website

BEYOND BENEFITS

Benefits are crucial, but don't forget practical matters. (See "Checklist for communications.") Include this information as much as possible in your written communications, but don't be surprised if you have to repeat it when you speak to people who've read your email/handbill/Facebook post/Instagram post.

Try to be brief (delete blather!) but provide needed detail. As much as possible, tailor your communications to your audience. Here's a slightly edited version of the copy I used in my initial prospecting email, whose audience was primarily middle-aged women whom I knew at least casually; borrow as you see fit.

Hi, [name],

After years of lifting and recent training as a coach, I'm ready to offer Olympic-style weight training classes, and I thought you might be interested. Lifting has increased my bone density (my original goal), and I am much stronger than when I started even though I am older. Why don't you join me in getting stronger, leaner, more powerful and more flexible?

Respond to this email or call XXX-XXX-XXXX to sign up now. Get in at half price if you sign up by March 15!

WHAT IT IS

This class teaches lifting for strength. It uses barbells as the primary equipment along with dumbbells as needed.

WHEN & WHERE

Classes meet twice a week, on Mondays and Wednesdays, at [address]. Maximum class size is nine.

I'm offering the following times. Class duration varies somewhat, depending on the workout, but generally runs 45–60 minutes.

Start times: 12 p.m., 4 p.m., and 5:30 p.m. (each class meets on both Monday and Wednesday)

Spring session: Mondays and Wednesdays, March 26 through May 17 (8 weeks)

Summer session: Mondays and Wednesdays, May 21 through August 8 (12 weeks, no class July 4)

FEES

Special introductory offer: The spring session will be just $XX—half price— for anyone signing up by March 15. After that, the fee is $XX.

Summer session: $XXX (12 weeks, minus July 4)

WHAT YOU NEED TO PARTICIPATE

You need to sign up in advance, and you need to wear comfortable clothes that allow freedom of movement. Sweatpants and a T-shirt, or anything you might wear for yoga, would be perfect, and basic athletic-type shoes. If you have a yoga mat, please bring it for abdominal exercises.

WHY THIS KIND OF STRENGTH TRAINING?

Olympic-style weightlifting works muscle groups, which means it not only builds strength, power, and flexibility, but it also:

—is time-efficient

—improves coordination

—strengthens the core

ABOUT ME

I'm 57 years old and I've been lifting since I was 50. Since then, my strength has soared and my bone density has increased without using pharmaceuticals. Until I started lifting, I didn't realize how much strength I'd lost. Among the unexpected benefits: I can hoist a bag of mulch or dog food with ease, and when I trip (me? a klutz?), I don't fall.

With my USA Weightlifting Level 1 coach certification, I'm eager to start this new venture to share this highly effective and fun program with you.

Respond to this email or call XXX-XXX-XXXX to sign up now or to ask questions. Get in at half price if you sign up by March 15! And please forward this message to anyone you know who might be interested.

Questions? Shoot me an email, give me a call, or see my website, http://givemestrength.net.

Thanks,
Janet Majure
USA Weightlifting Level 1 Coach
XXX-XXX-XXXX; coach@givemestrength.net

You will note that the letter includes some key elements of effective marketing and sales copy: a description of the program's **benefits** for the email recipient; a **discount**; a **deadline**; and **multiple requests for action**. Explaining the benefits tells the prospective client why she may want to try weightlifting; the deadline helps curtail procrastination (and forgetfulness); the requests for action tell them what they need to do; and, of course, everybody likes to get a deal. The important thing, of course, is that it worked.

Your specific message may be—probably will be—somewhat different, but this letter may give you a starting point for a flyer or email message. For me—and maybe for you if you are lucky—marketing by way of my personal network and word-of-mouth has been the name of the game. Word-of-mouth has many advantages: the prospective client is getting information from a source she trusts; the person spreading the word offers a live testimonial; and the client you wind up with is probably going to be pretty reliable (meaning pays fully and in a timely way), because he doesn't want his friend to think he's a jerk. Who knows? Maybe that client also will be motivated to stay, to be part of a group.

WEBSITES AND SOCIAL MEDIA

"Yeah, yeah," you say. "This is the 21st century. What about electronic media?" Two things: first, chances are exceedingly good that no one will find your website, at least initially, because they won't know it exists; and, two, social media is great only if your target audience uses it regularly. That said, I do recommend that you have a website that at the very least provides the same information as included in the letter above. These days, people expect most going concerns to have a website for reference.

You don't have to be a web expert to create a website, and various free options are available. My website, givemestrength.net, is powered by WordPress (the free software available at Wordpress.org) and hosted by Bluehost.com, and I am satisfied with both. You also can create a free site with zero experience at Wordpress.com, Wix.com, and Weebly.com, although you most likely will have to pay a small fee to have your own domain, such as example.com. I recommend WordPress for various reasons. Finding a desirable and available domain name may be the trickiest part. (See Appendix A for helpful tools.) For simplicity's sake, you may want to buy your domain name through your webhost.

As to social media, I have definitely gotten clients via Facebook, primarily (and possibly exclusively) due to my existing clients' recommendations there. If you have existing personal clients who would refer people to you from their Facebook status reports—with a link to your website or business Facebook page—that's excellent. Mostly, though, social media will be more useful after you are up and running.

If you already have a strong web presence, with hundreds or thousands of followers on Twitter or Instagram, then by all means promote your business there! Let your followers know well in advance of your plans. Build interest and momentum. Make your followers part of your process of finding a location, finding equipment, passing on your request for startup clients. Do the same on your personal Facebook page, and create a Facebook business page.

If you don't have a significant web presence, don't worry about it. You certainly can get your business up and running and making money without being a social media maven. I believe that most coaches and trainers will get most mileage in the beginning out of their personal in-person network and their good reputations. If you lack those, too, well, you may have a hard time.

GET STARTED NOW

As soon as you have decided you want to give it a go, start telling people your plans. Don't be surprised if friends and acquaintances offer to help, but at the same time don't hesitate to ask. Just say, "I'm starting a weightlifting business. Are you interested? If you know anyone who might be interested, please send them my way!" And be ready with answers, and perhaps that handbill mentioned previously, when they do.

CHAPTER 8

RUN YOUR CLASSES

In Chapter 4, you read about the workout program that your business will be based on plus suggested lift adaptations and progression as clients gain strength and skill. This chapter takes a look at how you and your clients keep records of their progress some of the practical matters that will come into play in your classes. As you go along, you will refine the process to a form that is right for you and your clients, but the practices explained here have worked for me for years, so they are a good place to start.

As you face your first recruits, you may see a group that is entirely new to weightlifting. Or maybe you have worked with some of them individually; others may have lifted weights with someone else or lifted when they were in high school 30 years earlier. No matter. It's a good plan to proceed similarly for everyone, knowing that the rate of progress will vary, which is going to be true regardless of your clients' experience. The only exception is if you have some experienced clients with established and current 1RMs and you are familiar with their skill level. Those, you can start on the periodized program as soon as you are sure of their ability.

Some of the information in this chapter may seem obvious or familiar if you've managed classes or several clients at a gym. Nevertheless, at least skim through it as you may come across some ideas that are new and useful to you.

APPROACH TO INSTRUCTION

We'll start with a few comments about teaching. The following information may be a reminder of things you already know, but it's nevertheless worth repeating.

First, remember that different people prefer different modes of learning. Thus, it's helpful to provide more than one mode of instruction, including describing the action, demonstrating it, and, best of all, having the client try to do it. If you have experienced lifters with good technique in your class, it's nice to be able to ask them to demonstrate, partly because you'll save your energy and partly because you will be able to point out things to clients as they watch in ways that you couldn't if you are the demonstrator. A few people may be disappointed if you (like me) don't provide mirrors. But for people who need some visual reinforcement of their own movement, it's easy to make a video with a smartphone to show them—and to send to them if they need it.

Second, be sure to point out what people are doing right. Doing so reinforces a movement pattern you are teaching, and it helps clients feel good about what they are doing. A few people may become easily discouraged by corrections, and remarking that they are doing a good job of keeping their back flat, for instance, lets them know they are making progress.

Third, you might want to work to develop multiple descriptions of the same movement. Different descriptions seem to resonate with different people.

When making a correction or a positive comment, be as specific as possible. A general "not like that" or "good job" isn't particularly instructive.

Instruction tips

- Allow for different learning styles.

- Point out what people are doing right.

- Make corrections and positive comments as specific as you can.

- Explain movements multiple ways.

WORKOUT RECORDS

Each class member needs to have a record of her workouts. I provide forms for that purpose, one form for new or novice clients and a different form for clients who have 1RMs. Appendix A provides links to sample forms (in Excel format) that you are welcome to use or to adapt. You may prefer to create your own forms, direct your clients to get a notebook for that purpose, or go another route altogether. But whatever approach you take, you and your clients need a record of:

- workout date;

- weight for each set; and

- number of repetitions for each set.

This information will allow you to observe progress and to plan future workouts. The novices' forms that I use provide spaces only for date and weight, as they complete 10-rep sets for their introductory period. For clients with established 1RMs, the forms provide spaces for the date, weight, number of reps, and a table that calculates weights for percentages of 1RM for each lift.

The examples you find in Appendix A are just two of probably countless options. My first coach kept a separate workout sheet for each lift. A quick Google search will reveal many other options. Just find something that is easy for your clients and easy for you.

Next, make sure someone—you or your clients—records the workouts. For experienced lifters, I write the day's workout on a whiteboard, and clients complete their own workout records.

For novice lifters, what has worked best in my studio is for me to record the workouts for the first few weeks while they learn the lifts. I'll observe them and add weight as appropriate. Once they develop a degree of knowledge and I feel confident of their ability, I may write down a recommended workout for them, and that recommended workout serves as their record unless the actual workout diverges from that plan for one reason or another. (Possibilities include more difficulty than anticipated on a given lift at a given weight, or the client showing up tired and sore from, say, a heavy day of garden work.)

RECORD MANAGEMENT: TWO APPROACHES

Although there are no doubt many ways to manage workout records, what follows are descriptions of two widely divergent approaches.

My first coach left clients entirely responsible for their own record keeping. They carried their workout records to and from the weight room; recorded the date, weight, and repetitions for each lift; recorded their 1RMs; and calculated the percentages of 1RMs as appropriate for the workout. He provided calculators and pens but never—or very rarely—looked at anyone's records. He might ask someone what her 1RM is on a particular lift or ask her how much she lifted on the previous workout, but that's about it. At the beginning of each class, he would announce the workout (although he gave everyone a copy of the complete program at the beginning of the session) and state variations as appropriate for individuals who had been absent or sick.

But here's another option. Perhaps, like me, you lack confidence in your ability either to remember who is where in the program or to announce workout adjustments on the fly. Also, even though I'm very comfortable with numbers, many people are not, and I don't want math anxiety to deter anyone from lifting. As a result, I rely on paper, not on my memory. I provide workout sheets for clients as noted above, and I have tiered letter trays (such as you might see in an office; see Appendix A for recommendations) where I keep workout sheets. The trays are sturdy and provide easy access. One tray serves one class, and clients pick up and return their sheets to their class tray/shelf. To simplify finding things, I assign a color to each class tray, and mark the top of each workout record with the appropriate class color.

Then, between classes, I review workout sheets. I write nothing on the sheets of people who are up to date on the session's workout program (they know to do the workout on the whiteboard), and I write "ask" for the next workout for someone who has been sick. If I expect someone to return to lifting after a vacation, I'll write the date of their return and their workout, if different from the class's.

Each approach has its pros and cons. You may want to take some other approach, and that's fine too.

Client-managed approach

PROS	CONS
Less paperwork for coach	Excellent memory (or other record) required for coach
No storage needed at gym	
Empowerment for clients to take charge of their lifting	Guesswork when clients forget to bring records
	Math challenges for clients

Coach-managed records

PROS	CONS
Coach up to date on clients' performance	Paperwork for coach
Less math anxiety for clients	Storage spot needed for workout records
Records stay at gym	Babying clients (though I've had no complaints!)

'CLASSROOM' MANAGEMENT

Your clients probably won't arrive at the same time or in the same state of readiness. Some people just seem inclined to arrive early or late, and others have scheduling or travel factors outside their control to consider. In any event, here's how things generally proceed once clients know the lifts: clients arrive, warm up, then do the workouts. If you provide the records, they also will pick up their workout sheets and, perhaps, write out the specific weights they'll do for each lift.

Classes typically last about an hour, but the time varies depending on how fast individuals lift, how adequately they rest between sets, how hard the day's workout may be, how experienced the lifters are. In theory, you have three lifters per platform, with one lifting and two resting and/or helping change plates as needed. In an ideal world, those three also would be of similar heights and lift similar amounts of weight and understand and enjoy sharing.

In the real world, however, people won't arrive at the same time, work at the same pace, stand at the same height, lift the same amount of weight, notice that anyone else is lifting, or do any number of other tasks in a uniform manner. The results can be frustrating for you, and sometimes for your lifters, too. Here are some scenarios to consider, most of which have the result of creating an imbalance in the availability of equipment.

Late arriver

Nell arrives 20 minutes late. She does her power cleans and push presses from blocks, as it's a moderate workout, and she's strong enough to lift the bar to her shoulders for push presses. When she's ready to squat, though, she wants to use a rack, but everybody else is doing Romanian deadlifts or bench presses from the racks.

Early arriver

Kim arrives 20 minutes early. The preceding class is just finishing up, so Kim proceeds to warm up and work out. She has a rack to herself for RDL while her eight classmates are doing squats or push presses on the other two racks.

Speed lifter

Joe arrives on time but he has his own agenda, namely to get done as fast as possible. He rushes his warm-up and does two of the three sets of power cleans before others are ready to start. He has a rack to himself doing bench presses while others are a looking for a rack for their RDLs.

Exclusive mates

Emily and Lynn are a good match in terms of height, amount of weight lifted, and so on, and they have developed a good rapport with each other—so good, in fact, that they have a tendency to forget or ignore the third person working out on the platform with them or unintentionally create a social barrier that deters others from asking to work in with them.

Proprietary rights

Most people will habitually work out at the same platform. Some will prefer certain plates or collars or bar cushions or bars. That's all OK until Jody gets upset because Casey is working on "her" platform or until Gene gets mad because he can't find his favorite collars. (If you have secondhand equipment, and maybe even with some new equipment, you will have variation.)

What to do?

Ultimately, you must decide for yourself how to manage these situations according to what works best for you, but here are some suggestions that may help:

Early or late arrival. You can have hard rules on this matter if you are willing to enforce them. I try to be at least somewhat flexible given that individuals' arrival times frequently are a product of when they get off work or unexpected traffic delays. Hence, my guidelines are that people who arrive early don't warm up or start their workouts while members of the preceding class are finishing up—unless those members are running late, meaning beyond the official starting time of the second class. If people arrive extra late, I generally suggest that they do the core work at home. (I do believe some actually follow through!) My first coach, whose gym was in his garage, had a rule that nobody started lifting until he entered, although they could warm up. That rule eliminated the problem of early arrivers getting far ahead of their classmates.

Speed lifting. This one can be tougher to manage. Some people seem to go through life in a hurry. Some can't bear resting. Some perhaps prefer not to share, and rationalize that by rushing they're getting out of the way of everyone else. Whatever the cause, it's a frustrating situation to manage. It's worthwhile to remind your clients of the value of resting—they'll get stronger, and that's why they're working out—but people in this category may not care. If your slower and less-assertive clients hang back waiting for the jackrabbit, you may need to step in and ask the speed lifter to step aside while someone else does a set, even if it means resetting the rack for a different lift.

Exclusive mates. I sense that most of these pairs don't mean to be standoffish, but they get sufficiently wrapped up in their conversations that they aren't really aware of others. Again, you may want to step in occasionally and suggest that so-and-so needs to work with them.

Proprietary rights. I keep it good-natured, but I remind everyone as often as necessary that they are my bars, my platforms, my racks—and no client has priority over any of them. It seems to work, although I did have to decline one client's request that I assign platforms to avoid interlopers on her (ahem!) platform.

In addition to these steps, you may find it worthwhile to start each multiweek session with reminders that resting is part of the program, that sharing is part of the program (not to mention the friendly and collegial thing to do) and easy when you need to be resting anyway. You may prefer to ignore these situations entirely and let clients work things out for themselves—or you may want to establish concrete rules for matters like these. I lean toward being accommodating as much as I can while trying to moderate the impulses of both the timid and the pushy.

DIMINISHING MENTAL ACUITY

You are helping your clients stay mentally sharp even as you are helping them to get physically strong, and there's much evidence to support that statement.[9] Nevertheless, if many of your clients are over, say, 60 years old, it's a fact of life that problems of diminishing mental acuity may arise. The challenges I've seen in the weight room have ranged from minor forgetfulness to disabling cognitive loss. And, of course, there are people whose reduced sharpness falls in the middle of these extremes. Let's talk a little about these situations, with the understanding that I'm not an expert in gerontology and am speaking from my experiences in the weight room.

At the forgetfulness end of the spectrum, you probably have nothing to worry about. Just expect that you may have to remind some clients at every other workout what is a power clean (for instance), or you may need to remind them the difference between reps and sets or occasionally help them remember how to load the bar. These aren't big problems, as the people in this category seem to recognize their forgetfulness and seek help. Reminding them to focus on the immediate task at hand isn't a bad idea, though.

Another general category includes those who may or may not seem particularly forgetful but their ability to follow relatively complex instructions can be a challenge. In particular, a subset of people may have difficulty parsing their workout instructions (a problem no doubt exacerbated by widespread fear of math). They may be able to figure out how much is 70% of their 1RM for their heaviest set, but they may not be clear on how much less to do in their first and second sets, or, probably worse (unless it turns out they were holding back when testing!), they do their first set at the designated maximum and then add weight. Some may get confused when the workout involves heavy lifting on three lifts and light on three lifts. Depending on your patience and the frustration level of the clients, you can coach them in filling out their workout plan for the day, or check their work, or simply fill in the required weights for each lift for them.

In cases of significant cognitive decline, clients may need enough assistance or supervision that they aren't able to manage in a group setting (or you aren't able to provide the necessary help). They may be better off with a personal trainer or working out in class with an aide. I've seen two such situations, at opposite ends of the weightlifting experience scale. In one case, a lifter who had been working out for close to 20 years exhibited significant confusion and became unable to determine how much weight to lift, to load the bar correctly, and to keep track of how many sets she had done. (Any of those may happen from time to time with normal memories, particularly when people get caught up in conversations, but they don't usually happen consistently and in combination.) Her actual lifting was good, though, as the movement patterns were well ingrained. In another case, a new lifter who could carry on conversations just fine (up to a point) was not able to learn the lifts because he simply could not retain information from one moment to the next, including how to execute the lifts.

I don't have any magic solutions to deal with these situations. Still, I mention them because you need to be aware that they probably will arise, and it is helpful to have some idea in advance of how you want to deal with it. So far, I haven't had to "fire" any clients because they've lost mental acuity, but that day may come, and I'm not looking forward to it.

NEW AND RETURNING LIFTERS

Chances are that at first all of your clients will be new to lifting and as a result will require considerable instruction and close supervision. (That's one reason not to feel bad if your first class or two isn't full.) If you're providing instruction and encouragement and people are feeling stronger, they'll return for subsequent sessions.

Then, you may have a mix of experienced and new lifters. That's an advantage for your instruction of both old and new clients. You will be able to point to current clients as examples for the novices to emulate, and current clients get a refresher course in technique as they listen in. Meanwhile, in the first few weeks of a new session, you will devote much or most of your attention to the new people, and the experienced people will carry on in the background. Your role eventually evolves to where you are keeping an eye on all clients during their lifts and providing pointers to improve their lifts, their focus, and their safety.

Eventually, you may have multiple classes with only returning clients. Chapter 9 talks more about how to maintain those clients' interest and skills.

ABSENCES AND SUBSTITUTIONS

One of the most crucial factors in strength-building success is working out consistently. As a result, I do all I can to encourage clients to work out twice a week. To that end, I try to make the environment serve their needs, and remind them that making a habit of working out makes attendance easier than making decisions twice a week about whether to go. (Inner dialog in the former case: "It's Monday and I'm tired. But I work out at 4 on Mondays. Better take my gear." Inner dialog in the latter: "Should I go? I'm tired. Maybe I'll skip. Then I'll feel guilty, and then Wednesday will be harder. I don't know. Oh, I should have left 10 minutes ago. Guess I'll stay home.")

Possibly the most important way that I encourage clients to attend regularly is by allowing them to substitute into other classes as space permits—and assuming they allow at least a day between workouts. I've opted for a manual approach—no computer required for clients—and you may want to go that route, too.

The chief advantage for a manual approach is that clients like it. Happy clients are returning clients. It's easy for them just to tell me in person—or via text message, telephone, or email—that they are going to miss and that they'd like to find a different spot. I've asked if they'd rather be able to go online and record absences and request time changes, and the answer has been an emphatic no; much easier (for them) just to tell me.

The chief disadvantages are to me: I am subject to messages of various sorts at all times, and I have to devise and maintain a method to keep track. I've tried two methods. The first is essentially a spreadsheet (in Appendix A, see link to an example) on copy paper with spaces for each class period and columns labeled "Out," "In," and "Wants In." When someone advises me that she is going to be out of town on a given date, I record the name in the Out column for her class. If someone from another class needs to work out at that time, his name goes in the In column (and in the Out column for his own class). If someone wants to work out at a given time and I don't have an opening, I record the name in the Wants In column and then advise that person if an opening develops. It isn't pretty or elegant, but it works.

Unfortunately, this paper record may not be particularly convenient for carrying around. One solution to that is to take a photo with my mobile phone so that I can refer to it when clients contact me when I am away from the studio. I then use sticky notes or phone reminders to myself to change the record when I return to the studio. It usually works, but no one would call it elegant.

As I write this, I'm trying an alternative paper record that's handy for carrying around, and it's working well. I purchased a thin, pocket-sized notebook (see Appendix A for suggestions) and manually created a substitutions record with the same arrangement as the spreadsheet, only much smaller. To save space, I marked each class section with its color rather than write in the times. This approach forces me to write small, but that's a small price. I keep it with me pretty much at all times by mentally associating it with my mobile telephone.

GETTING BACK UP TO SPEED

Of course, substitutions don't help much for people who head out on three-week vacations or who stay home sick for two days or who miss one workout a week for three consecutive weeks due to a work backlog. If someone who is up to speed misses a single workout, that person generally can simply resume the workout series you have planned.

In the other situations, you will need to adjust the workouts. I know of no hard-and-fast rule for doing so, but in general those who have been absent get a workout that has lower volume or intensity (compared with those who've been working out regularly) or, sometimes, both. Workout reductions are greater for those who have been sickest or have been gone the longest (unless they were working out while away), and the older the client the gentler you may want to be in returning them to form. Better to err on the side of too easy than too hard for someone returning after an absence. Maintaining a dialog with such a lifter during the first and second workouts after his return will provide guidance.

FROM DAY-TO-DAY TO LONG TERM

This chapter has focused on the day-to-day concerns of operating your classes. The next chapter will focus on what we might call the macrocycle of your weight-lifting business. That is, it will look at activities that you may want to undertake to engage, educate, and train your clients over the long term.

CHAPTER 9

KEEPING CLIENTS ENGAGED

Remarkably enough, considering we do the same lifts in every workout, clients don't complain about this program getting boring. Why? Just getting the technique right to lift well and safely continues to require focus, the social aspect keeps their interest, and the cyclical changing of volume and intensity creates a feeling of more variety than you might think. Just the same, you don't want clients to slip into bad habits or bad form as familiarity sets in. Your clients' advancement allows and even requires your shifting from strictly teaching to a greater emphasis on coaching and expanding or improving clients' knowledge. This fact means the workouts don't become boring for you, either!

The overall strategy for keeping clients engaged essentially is one of continuing education. I use three approaches to that end: periodic "refresher courses" on various lifts or parts of lifts, a newsletter, and workshops or special events. You don't have to dive into any of these as you're getting started, but they're good tools to use as you get established.

REFRESHERS

You may want to be systematic—or not—about providing refresher instruction. Since my classes these days are more than 90% returnees, I provide some added such instruction at some point in most sessions, but I'm inconsistent and clients don't seem to mind. My refreshers involve detailed descriptions of technique plus demonstrations. The topics may cover just one small aspect of a lift—say the first pull of a power clean—or they may be an entire lift, especially for simpler lifts. Depending on time constraints and clients' needs, you potentially could ask each client to demonstrate the item you've just reviewed or simply ask clients to make that item of particular focus for them that week.

In my classes, the reviews tend to run in series. I might review one lift a week for six weeks, or once a week for several weeks I might review one part of the power clean. Whatever the teaching focus of a given refresher, be sure to reinforce the lesson by watching clients as they perform the lift and commenting on their correct technique.

NEWSLETTER

A newsletter can further promote connections between you and your clients as well as provide another teaching tool. Among the methods you could use are making simple photocopies to hand out or make available in your gym; an email newsletter; or blog posts or articles on your website. I lean toward the email or handout approaches, as they require no effort on the part of your audience apart from reading. Blog posts and website articles first require the client to make a decision to go to the website.

A newsletter doesn't have to be fancy, but you and your business will look more professional if it at least uses clear writing with good grammar and spelling. (Hey, my first career was as an editor!) I recommend emphasizing useful and interesting information rather than sending out a sales brochure in disguise. The idea is to inform and connect with your clients. Regular features might include:

- clients' anniversaries with your business
- introductions of new clients
- farewell to old clients
- profile of one client (with photo)
- calendar of session dates, holidays, and so on
- notices or explanation of new policies, equipment, features
- coach's comments

The feedback I get suggests that the anniversaries, profile, and coach's comments are the most popular. Anniversaries are self-explanatory, although I might note that I go by session start date—for example, spring 2014—rather than a calendar date for determining anniversaries. And I don't have a good method of accounting for people who leave and then come back. (If you know of one, let me know!) The profiles are pretty basic: name, age, how long lifting, favorite lift and why, least favorite lift and why, what they get out of lifting. I try to vary the profiles by class, experience, age, and sex so that readers are likely to see someone they know or someone like themselves in the profiles.

"Coach's comments" means a short(ish) article about some topic that I want to explain more fully (such as why I started teaching push press in front of instead of behind the neck) or a topic that clients frequently ask about (such as what they can do while traveling to try to maintain their strength) or some general principle that may get lost in the noise (such as how muscle gets stronger). As you no doubt have observed, the fitness world is awash in conflicting information and exercise fads, and occasionally those serve as the starting points for an article.

I send email newsletters using MailChimp, which has a free version, because I can make them look nicer than a basic email and it's a convenient list manager, but you may prefer something such as a Word document (or save as a PDF) that you print out, or copy and paste into an email, or attach to an email. If writing or web-based newsletter design and distribution is outside your comfort zone, just keep it simple.

Incidentally, although I do have a website and a business Facebook page, they do not take the place of the newsletter, which is more personal than the web information. See Chapter 10 for a little about those marketing venues.

WORKSHOPS, SPECIAL EVENTS, AND MORE

Workshops and special events may help maintain clients' positive attitudes about your business, provide education, support a charity, or simply be fun. This sort of thing tends to take more effort on your part with less-clear benefits to your business and to your clients than the refresher lessons and newsletters. Nevertheless, if you love this sort of thing, here's a brief introduction to these goodwill-inducing possibilities. When I have done them, clients consistently have liked them and participated.

Workshop. A workshop is an event with a specific educational component. It might be open to all clients, to a specific category of clients, or to clients and their friends. It could be free of charge, or you could charge a fee. One workshop I offered provided good demonstrations with commentary outside the demands of a workout. Clients with good technique demonstrated (by invitation) one lift apiece, and a visiting, experienced lifter demonstrated the competition lifts and explained how our workouts related to them. Other possibilities: a hands-on workshop where you drill power clean technique; a "weightlifting recital" in which clients could take turns performing (or showing off!) their favorite lifts for friends and family; a body mechanics expert to provide tips on safe lifting.

Charity workout. Our studio participated in a cancer fund-raiser. Clients raised money for the American Cancer Society and then participated in a free, extra workout, complete with snacks and prizes.

Social gatherings. My first coach had an annual potluck picnic for all clients and significant others, which was well attended. From time to time I've arranged for a cocktail hour on the patio of a restaurant near the studio. These reinforce the social connections people make in class, and everyone seems to have fun.

And more. You can use your creativity to come up with other ideas to engage your clients. I give out gold stars at the beginning of each session to people marking anniversaries, and I also have "good job!" type of stickers that I put on workout sheets occasionally. I've been both amused and pleased by how much people seem to like these. Also, at least three-fourths of my clients bought T-shirts with the business name and web address on the front (plus a quote about strength on the back) when I had them made two or three years ago, and I'm getting requests for a new batch. You might choose differently, but I sold them pretty much at cost, as I was more interested in clients' owning them than in making money off the T-shirts.

On a perhaps more-useful note, I keep a small supply on hand of two publications, which you can order free of charge from the National Institutes of Health (see Appendix A), about knee and shoulder problems. Clients have appreciated them. In addition, I wrote and distributed a booklet, "Secrets from the Weight Room," which provides some humor along with helpful tips for both new and returning clients.

PERSONAL TOUCH

Your business will do best when you remember that you are there to help your clients get strong and to do so in a way that helps them to feel supported. To that end, it's good to keep track, at least in your head, of your clients' infirmities, whether it's a troublesome knee, or a tendency to favor one arm, or a fear of back injury. Your workout instructions, of course, will take these matters into consideration, but people appreciate it if you check in with them from time to time about how that knee is feeling. The key advantages you have over a standard gym is the personal attention you offer and at a price significantly less than a personal trainer.

CHAPTER 10

PROMOTE AND EXPAND THE BUSINESS

Once you are up and running, once you feel confident of your systems and your clients are getting results, you are ready to start expanding your business. Now, more than ever, is where your good reputation and your clients' satisfaction really count. This chapter talks about how to encourage your clients to renew and to make referrals, plus some other ideas on how you can expand.

A good progression for your business would go something like this: start with a couple of classes, probably not full; fill or nearly fill those classes; add and partly fill another class or two; fill those and then add more if you want. When you reach a number of classes that feels right for you, you can expand further by hiring another coach to lead classes.

I stopped adding classes when I had seven, each meeting twice a week. That number allows me plenty of time to do the administrative functions without working more hours than I want. If I were younger, I might add another class or two—the market exists—but this feels like a good number to me, and I don't want to teach classes at 7 a.m. or 7 p.m. (A prospective client I was chatting with once asked whether my 5:30 class was a.m. or p.m. I laughed and assured her that the only thing I do at 5:30 a.m. is sleep. But she was disappointed—and I'm missing the early bird market.)

In the last couple of years, my business has expanded indirectly. I wanted to make classes available to more people—especially as I was having to turn away clients—without having to teach them myself. I knew a younger lifter who teaches water fitness classes, and her students praise her teaching. I asked if she was interested in teaching weightlifting. She was and took the USA Weight-lifting Level 1 coaching course. After some discussion, she decided she would rather start her own business at my gym than hire on as an employee. We worked out the details, and she now has two weightlifting classes at my gym—and I lift in one of them!

RENEWING CURRENT CLIENTS

I want my current clients to have a good experience, and I want them to come back. They are and always have been my core clients. In addition to keeping them engaged, as discussed in Chapter 9, I encourage their renewals in several ways. First, I try to make sure the class is filling their strength-building needs and desires and, as noted elsewhere, that includes being flexible when possible as to when they work out. Second, when I am signing people up for the next session, clients get priority up to a deadline date. That means, if they sign up by the deadline, I guarantee them a spot in their current class. It also means that if they need to switch to a different class time, they are first in line for any opening.

Other ways to build goodwill and keep renewals is to allow a partial session to clients who are going to be out of town for an extended period—but only if you are not fully subscribed. Also, you can allow payment plans for clients who can't pay the full tab up front. I often have a client or two who need to make such arrangements, and that's fine with me, although it does present a challenge to make sure neither I nor the client overlooks subsequent payments. Accepting credit cards can be another possible convenience both for you and your clients, although it has a cost-benefit profile that isn't worth it for me. You may feel otherwise.

ADDING CLASSES

If your intention is to grow a thriving weightlifting business, then you will want to add another class or two once you feel that your first classes are humming along—and more classes again later. To a certain extent you probably must go with your gut as to when that time is, particularly if adding a weightlifting class means cutting back on other jobs you may have. Still, it's a good sign when you have a waiting list for clients who want to get into your current classes, or when you don't offer classes at times that work for some people, such as that early bird crowd I mentioned.

When you think you are ready to add another class, your newsletter, your Facebook page, and any other social media you use will let you publicize your plan and encourage people to contact you. No need to fill a new class; if everyone is new, a small class often will be more manageable for you. Following are some suggestions on filling those classes.

GETTING REFERRALS

Whereas your number one source of clients when you started out most likely was your and your friends' networks, your clients' networks become a major referral source once you've been operating for a while. Your satisfied clients are your very best and most credible sources of referrals. I treasure the multiple clients who have referred five or more people who have signed up and stayed.

Naturally, I encourage those kinds of referrals. I do so not just by asking clients to share my information with their friends and family but also by reminding them that I'll pay them $10 (or reduce their fee by that amount) for anyone they refer who winds up as a client. Obviously, $10 isn't a huge amount, but it's enough that people appreciate it, and it beats the heck out of paid advertising. Incidentally, I've also had clients tell me thanks, but they don't need the reward; they are just happy that their friend is lifting.

My Facebook business page helps with getting referrals in that clients who are active on Facebook mention weightlifting from time to time and refer their friends to my Facebook page. I also post news items occasionally on Facebook about research that shows benefits of weightlifting or strength in general as well as links about weightlifting competitions in the area. Facebook provides another tool to reach prospective as well as current clients.

Just as with getting your first clients, you should take advantage of your Twitter or Instagram activity, if you use those services, to encourage more referrals.

GETTING PUBLICITY

Don't for a minute forget "old media," particularly local newspapers and television stations. I don't mean buy advertising; I mean get yourself in the newspaper as well as on television and radio. If you are of the mind-set that nobody pays attention to these things any more, think again. Although those sources have diminished among the overall population, they remain huge, especially with your target demographic. Remember, older people get more of their news from television than people of other ages, and lots of the news that people are getting (and sharing) online comes from the same institutions that publish the newspapers.[10][11] Thus, the internet magnifies the publicity that you get on old media. And, of course, you can post links to the coverage on your web page and social media accounts.

In many ways, your business has the hallmarks of the kind of feature story news outlets love. It's positive, it's unusual, it has good visuals (videos! photos!), and it's related to health. The health care industry is a major source of advertising dollars to various news outlets, and those outlets like to include health-related information, partly as a result.

You can read a book or two on how to get publicity in newspapers and broadcast media, but it's probably not required. The main thing to do is to identify a print or broadcast reporter who seems to cover fitness or health topics, and then contact that person. It's good to remember a couple of things: the reporter you contact is always looking for good story ideas, and that reporter is a very busy person. Therefore, be polite, enthusiastic, and brief. It's helpful to have a couple of very specific suggestions, especially suggestions that tie you and your business into bigger or national news topics. For instance:

"You may have read about the study that showed weightlifting reduces depression, and I thought you might like to talk to me or my clients about the mood benefits of the weightlifting we do here with mature adults using barbells."

"I saw you had a story about the drawbacks of bodybuilding, and I thought you might be interested in seeing what weightlifting is about—which is different from bodybuilding—and its health benefits."

"I saw your story regarding concerns about elderly people falling, and I thought your readers might like to see that there's something most older people can do about it."

These are examples of brief, to-the-point pitches you might make. Reporters like getting email pitches, and you could try placing a telephone call. Again, be brief. Whatever you do, provide your telephone number or numbers, your email address, your website address (if you have a site), and your business's social media link, if you have one.

You probably won't score coverage with every reporter or editor or producer you contact, but contacting them is definitely worth a shot. And if you hit, you likely will get many more inquiries than you do by networking. That means two things: you'd better have at least some openings you want to fill, and you need to understand that these leads don't come "prequalified" in the way your network-won contacts do. Hence, expect to answer a lot of questions and spend a fair amount of time talking to these potential clients to make sure they understand what you do and to make sure their expectations are realistic.

ADDING PERSONNEL

Hiring people adds a significant amount of complexity, but it's almost the only way to grow (if that's your desire) without your teaching more classes. At the very least, having an employee (or employees) means you will have to account for and pay for income tax withholding, Social Security and Medicare withholdings (both of which you will match), unemployment taxes, and, probably, workers' compensation insurance. And you will need to schedule and supervise your employee(s). All of these tasks are entirely doable, but they can be a pain in the neck, and you need to do them right so that you don't get sideways with the tax collector. Check with your nearest Small Business Development Center (see https://www.sba.gov/tools/local-assistance/sbdc) for information on federal, state, and local employer information.

SUBLEASING

There is an alternative to hiring, however, which is why I said hiring is "almost" the only way to expand. This alternative probably won't make as much money for you as hiring an employee, but it is certainly easier and carries little financial risk. I was planning to hire someone because I wanted to make lifting available to more people, and I knew that I didn't want to lead more classes. But my likely hire, Colleen, decided that she'd rather rent space and equipment from me and have her own business. That option had a greater upside potential for her.

She now teaches two weightlifting classes, and pays me a flat fee for each. I consulted my landlord and insurance provider and got the OK. I provide the space, equipment, paper supplies, cleaning, and so on. She collects her own fees, carries her own business liability insurance, sets her schedule working around my classes, and designs her own program. It's worked out great for both of us, and she's my coach these days.

Incidentally, I would discourage you from trying to skirt taxes by bringing someone on as a contractor following your directions so as to spare you the tax expense and inconvenience. Doing so isn't just unethical but also illegal, and could be a bad decision in the long run. You can read the IRS guidance, "Understanding Employee vs. Contractor Designation," at https://www.irs.gov/newsroom/understanding-employee-vs-contractor-designation, or talk to your accountant or lawyer.

OTHER SIDE OPTIONS

If you want or need to make added money from this business, other options are available. You could offer one-on-one coaching; I've had a number of inquiries but it isn't really what I want to do. Depending on how you are set up, you could rent space to trusted colleagues for leading other kinds of fitness classes; you just need to make sure the terms work well for you. You could sell related products, keeping in mind that pushing products might turn off some clients.

THE LONGER TERM

What's next? It's up to you. I do believe that if you are entrepreneurial and focused on expanding, the potential for growth definitely is there. In the world of fitness, this is a highly unusual program in that it provides real, measurable results that can significantly improve quality of life, and it isn't a gimmick or a fad or something that abuses your body. People, especially those over 40 or 50 years old, appreciate those factors.

But your business doesn't have to get big. If you like having a steady income without the headaches of being part of a large organization—either as an employee or as its leader—you might be happy coaching a loyal group of clients. If you do well, there's also the potential for you to sell the business if you want to retire or simply move on to something else. Nothing wrong with that as a long-term goal!

I hope you give this program a go. Programs of this type simply are not widely available despite the huge value they have to clients. Start small if you can (and thus avoid debt) and then grow a loyal and grateful following. Or, in weightlifting terms, develop a strong core, and that makes the rest of the work easier and more effective.

Acknowledgments

My business and this book resulted from the contributions and support of many people, and I am endlessly grateful for their help:

Loren McVey, my first weightlifting coach, for teaching me how to lift and encouraging me to start my own business.

Neil Salkind, my dearly missed friend, neighbor, collaborator, cheerleader, and agent, who pushed me for years to write a book about weightlifting. I wish he had lived long enough to see it happen.

Susan Lee, my beloved daughter, whose determination sets a fine example for me and who gave the book's title its final nudge.

My first clients (including several who just keep coming back, bless them), who took a chance on me.

My current clients, who make it all worthwhile. Two of them, Carolyn Crawford and Angela Candela, get special thanks for sending so many other clients my way (in addition to sticking with me since 2012). Angela and Michael Morley also get thanks for helping me out with countless upkeep details.

The clients who agreed to be photographed for the cover, in alphabetical order: Valerie Giedinghagen, Jerry Harper, Marilyn Hull, Amy Lee, and Toni Wills.

The wonderfully talented editorial and creative people who helped produce this book: Lynn Byczynski, Linda Finestone, Amanda Warren Martin (www.amandawarren.com), Karen Johnson, and Earl Richardson (www.earlrichardson.com). I can't recommend any of them enough.

Thanks also to Mark Van Vliet, for helping me get equipment; to Dave Dierker for letting me use his space at the outset; and to Colleen Boley, who is starting her own business at my facility. May it continue to grow strong!

Appendix A: Resources

This appendix provides information, mostly annotated internet links, to supplement what you have read in the text. **If you would like live links, rather than have to type in the URLs, go to http://janetmajure.com/strong/resources, where this list appears with live links.** Please keep in mind that links and web content are constantly changing, so I can't guarantee that the information I refer to will still be there when you check. Some links may result in the author receiving a small commission on purchases.

Chapter 2

Lifting videos

I don't necessarily endorse all that you may see on these videos, and there's a good chance that they will be different by the time you read this book. Nevertheless, here are some suggestions:

Training videos on USA Weightlifting website: https://www.teamusa.org/usa-weightlifting/weightlifting101/instructional-videos. [Note: USAW links not working at publication time.]

Competition videos from the International Olympics Committee: https://www.olympic.org/videos/weightlifting/

Chapter 4

Health assessments

Physical Activity Readiness Questionnaire (Canadian Society for Exercise Physiology, 2002 revision), http://givemestrength.net/wp-content/uploads/2018/02/par-q.pdf

Physical Activity Readiness Questionnaire (National Academy of Sports Medicine version), https://www.nasm.org/docs/default-source/PDF/nasm_par-q-(pdf-21k).pdf

Get Active Questionnaire, http://www.csep.ca/CMFiles/GAQ_CSEPPATHReadiness-Form_2pages.pdf

Get Active Questionnaire – Reference Document: Advice on What to Do If You Have a Yes Response, http://www.csep.ca/CMFiles/publications/GAQ_ReferenceDoc_2pages.pdf

Chapter 6

How to build a weightlifting platform

http://athleticlab.com/build-weightlifting-platform/

https://www.catalystathletics.com/article/1895/How-to-Build-a-Weightlifting-Platform/

How to build jerk blocks

http://www.eng.auburn.edu/~simonrl/wl/jerkboxes/

Equipment suppliers

Retailers of Olympic weightlifting equipment seem to come and go. The following suppliers have been around at least a few years and have at least a modest selection of bars and plates available. They are listed for your convenience, but their inclusion is not an endorsement. I would, however, recommend a supplier that understands and/or specializes in weightlifting equipment versus general "strength-training" equipment. The latter may not understand the needs specific to Olympic-type lifts. Do read the discussion in Chapter 5 before buying bars.

On the other hand, equipment not specific to weightlifting may be purchased from numerous stores and online vendors and secondhand. These items include standard bars, standard plates, and steel or iron plates for Olympic bars.

Olympic bars and plates, new

https://www.gopherperformance.com/strength/weightlifting-bars

https://www.roguefitness.com/weightlifting-bars-plates/barbells

https://www.getrxd.com/weightlifting.html

Power racks and similar

https://www.gopherperformance.com/strength/racks

https://www.roguefitness.com/rogue-rigs-racks/power-racks

Other exercise equipment, new

This category includes standard bars, plates, dumbbells, ankle weights, and exercise/yoga mats. You can find these at most any discount retailer or sporting goods store, including Dick's Sporting Goods, Sears, Amazon.com, and Walmart. I've had very good success finding yoga mats and some smaller dumbbells and weighted balls at T.J. Maxx.

Bars and plates (used)

I recommend new Olympic bars. The only secondhand bars I'd buy are those I could look at and feel, preferably in a lift or two. I bought a couple of crummy bars secondhand—before I realized the difference. Unless you're looking for competition-grade gear, though, you can buy decent plates at garage sales or online:

- http://craigslist.org
- http://ebay.com

Stall mats

https://www.tractorsupply.com/tsc/store-locator

Equipment reviews

https://garagegymbuilder.com/reviews-best-olympic-barbells/

http://www.garagegymreviews.com/best-olympic-barbell/

https://blog.adamantbarbell.com/420/best-olympic-weightlifting-bars/

Plate colors

The color scheme for Olympic plates per the International Weightlifting Federation (at http://www.iwf.net/weightlifting_/equipment/):

25 kg red

20 kg blue

15 kg yellow

10 kg green

5 kg white

2.5 kg red

2 kg blue

1.5 kg yellow

1 kg green

0.5 kg white

1RM calculations

Various app options exist for both Android and iOS. Check the reviews, and choose the one that fits your needs best. I am not recommending a specific one, as the basic one I used (and basic was all I wanted) wasn't maintained, and I've reverted to using a printed table. I think I like it more anyway, as I don't have to fiddle with my phone when testing. Following are links to a PDF and an Excel spreadsheet of a 1RM table. You can adapt the Excel table to suit your needs.

- PDF: http://givemestrength.net/wp-content/uploads/2018/02/1RM.pdf
- Excel (for Mac or Windows): http://givemestrength.net/wp-content/uploads/2018/02/1rm.xlsx

Chapter 7

Marketing resources

Amazon.com's list of small-business marketing best sellers: https://amzn.to/2v37vMn

Amazon.com's list of internet marketing books: https://amzn.to/2Ob1dCT

Amazon.com's list of social media marketing books: https://amzn.to/2A1sB3h

Melinda Emerson's list of 10 books on marketing for small businesses: https://succeed-asyourownboss.com/10-best-small-business-marketing-books-everyone-read/

A quick list of marketing ideas and links to related articles on The Balance website: https://www.thebalance.com/budget-friendly-business-promotion-2948441

Websites

Free website hosts and site builders: Wordpress.com, Wix.com, Weebly.com

Free website software: Wordpress.org

Web hosting (including free automatic WordPress.org software installation): Bluehost.com

Domain name generators: Panabee.com, Nameboy.com, Namemesh.com

Chapter 8

Workout recording forms

The one I use: http://givemestrength.net/wp-content/uploads/2018/07/liftrecord-master.xlsx

Notebooks

Thin pocket notebooks for substitutions: Ooly Pocket Pal journal, about 3 1/2" by 5" by 1/8" thick; Moleskine Cahier journal, about 3 3/8" by 5 3/8" by 3/16"; or Volant journal, 2 5/8" by 4 3/16" x 1/8". If you misplace things (as I do), go for something brightly colored that will stand out amid the clutter. The Moleskines are more durable. All are more durable and less bulky than throw-away spiral notebooks.

Chapter 9

The complete list of joint-related publications from the National Institute of Arthritis and Musculoskeletal and Skin Diseases is available here: https://catalog.niams.nih.gov/subject.cfm?SearchType=Category&Category=8. The two I keep on hand are "Questions and Answers about Knee Problems" and "Questions and Answers about Shoulder Problems."

Appendix B: Core

Following is a list of abdominal and back exercises that may be of use to you, or you may have others you prefer. They are offered as a starting point. Those without any kind of notes are in widespread use and presumably need no explanation. If you require one, just do a Google search. Unless otherwise noted, all are performed on the floor.

- Feet-on-bench crunch (lie on back with feet on bench, knees and hips at 90-degree angles; curl shoulders up; lie back and repeat)
- Bench knee pull-in (seated on end of bench and supporting upper body by grasping bench behind torso; lean back and extend legs, then pull knees to chest; repeat)
- Bicycle
- Bridge (yoga type)
- Bum balance (sit with knees bent; lean back and lift feet off floor so as to balance on backside; known in yoga as boat pose)
- Cancan (get in bridge position; raise one leg, then the other)
- Crunch
- Double crunch (curl shoulders up, and curl bent knees to chest)
- Elbow-to-opposite-knee crunch (on back; hands at head; knees bent, with ankle of one leg over knee of other leg, resulting in one knee pointing away from body; curl up and bring elbow across body to knee that is pointing outward; do set for one leg up, then a second set for the other leg)
- Flutter kick (on back, hands under pelvis, legs extended; alternately raise legs from hip, as if swimming; easier version: do with bent knees)
- Hip hop (legs straight overhead, arms to side; use abs—not momentum—and attempt to raise derriere from floor)
- Leg lift (extend legs and put hands under pelvis, then raise legs about 18 inches, repeat; for weaker backs, start with legs straight and overhead, then lower toward floor just before back starts to yield)
- Legs-up crunch with twist (on back; legs straight and held overhead; crunch up and bring elbow across to opposite knee)
- Plank
- Pointer (also known as bird dog)
- Pump crunch (like double crunch, except extend legs on each repetition, ideally not putting heels on floor)
- Reverse crunch (start in sitting up position, and then curl down)

- Standing side bend with dumbbell
- Side plank
- Smiley (on back, legs extended, hands under hips to support low back; move feet from side to side in a wide arc, as a pendulum, drawing an imaginary smile in the air)
- Superhero aka superman
- Upside-down toe touch (on back with legs straight overhead and arms extended in front of face, raise shoulders and reach for toes)
- Weighted twist (seated with knees bent; tuck elbows at sides and hold weight in front of torso at about waist level; lean back till torso is about at a 45-degree angle relative to the floor; rotate torso side to side; feet/ankles may be held down by partner or held in place by slipping feet under a fixed bar, or, alternatively, the exerciser can balance on hips with feet off floor)
- Wiper (start on back with legs straight overhead and arms extended to side; move legs to floor on alternate sides, in the fashion of the movement of a windshield wiper; easier version: do with bent knees)

Notes

1   Belanger, Steve. "Confessions of a Middle-Aged CrossFit Newbie," January 5, 2015. https://www.huffingtonpost.com/steve-belanger-/confessions-of-a-middleag_b _6412522.html. Accessed July 2, 2018.

2   Statistic Brain Research Institute. "Gym Membership Statistics," August 30, 2017. https://www.statisticbrain.com/gym-membership-statistics/. Accessed December 13, 2017.

3   FirstResearch. "Fitness Centers," October 9, 2017. Retrieved from First Research database on December 15, 2017.

4   Averkamp, Stephanie. "Gym statistics: members, equipment, and cancellations." http://www.fitnessforweightloss.com/gym-statistics-members-equipment-and-cancellations/. Accessed July 13, 2018. Quoting from IHRSA report.

5   Berger, M.J. and T.J. Doherty. "Sarcopenia: Prevalence, Mechanisms, and Functional Consequences," 94–114, in *Body Composition and Aging*. Basel, Switzerland: Karger, 2010. https://doi.org/10.1159/000319997. Volume 37 in series, *Interdisciplinary Topics in Gerontology*.

6   *Physical Activity Guidelines Advisory Committee Report, 2008: To the Secretary of Health and Human Services*. Washington, D.C.: U.S. Dept. of Health and Human Services, 2008. http://www.health.gov/PAGuidelines. Details for this note found at https://health.gov/paguidelines/report/g5_musculo.aspx#_Toc199945425.

7   USA Weightlifting. "Olympic Lifting College Courses." https://www.teamusa.org/ USA-Weightlifting/Coaching/Olympic-Lifting-College-Courses. Accessed December 20, 2017.

8   USA Weightlifting. "University Programs." https://www.teamusa.org/USA-Weight-lifting/Clubs-LWC/University-Programs. Accessed December 20, 2017.

9   Northey J.M., N. Cherbuin, K.L. Pumpa, et al. Northey, Joseph Michael, Nicolas Cherbuin, Kate Louise Pumpa, Disa Jane Smee, and Ben Rattray. "Review: Exercise interventions for cognitive function in adults older than 50: a systematic review with meta-analysis." British Journal of Sports Medicine, 2018. Vol 52:154-160. http://dx.doi.org/10.1136/bjsports-2016-096587.

10   Gottfried, Jeffrey and Elisa Shearer. "Americans' online news use is closing in on TV news use." http://www.pewresearch.org/fact-tank/2017/09/07/americans-online-news-use-vs-tv-news-use/. Accessed June 8, 2018.

11   Shearer, Elisa and Jeffrey Gottfried. "News Use Across Social Media Platforms 2017." http://www.journalism.org/2017/09/07/news-use-across-social-media-platforms-2017/. Accessed June 8, 2018.

Works Cited and Further Reading

Averkamp, Stephanie. "Gym statistics: members, equipment, and cancellations." http://www.fitnessforweightloss.com/gym-statistics-members-equipment-and-cancellations/. Accessed July 13, 2018. Quoting from IHRSA report.

Belanger, Steve. "Confessions of a Middle-Aged CrossFit Newbie," January 5, 2015. https://www.huffingtonpost.com/steve-belanger-/confessions-of-a-middleag_b_6412522.html. Accessed July 2, 2018.

Berger, M.J. and T.J. Doherty. "Sarcopenia: Prevalence, Mechanisms, and Functional Consequences," 94–114, in Body Composition and Aging. Basel, Switzerland: Karger, 2010. https://doi.org/10.1159/000319997. Volume 37 in series, Interdisciplinary Topics in Gerontology.

Brady, Anne O. and Chad R. Straight. "Muscle capacity and physical function in older women: What are the impacts of resistance training?" Journal of Sport and Health Science 3 (September 2014), 179–188. doi.org/10.1016/j.jshs.2014.04.002.

Contreras, Bret and Brad Schoenfeld. "To Crunch or Not to Crunch: An Evidence-Based Examination of Spinal Flexion Exercises, Their Potential Risks, and Their Applicability to Program Design," Strength and Conditioning Journal 33 (August 2011): 8–18. doi: 10.1519/SSC.0b013e3182259d05

FirstResearch. "Fitness Centers," October 9, 2017. Retrieved from First Research database on December 15, 2017.

Gottfried, Jeffrey and Elisa Shearer. "Americans' online news use is closing in on TV news use." http://www.pewresearch.org/fact-tank/2017/09/07/americans-online-news-use-vs-tv-news-use/. Accessed June 8, 2018.

Northey J.M., N. Cherbuin, K.L. Pumpa, et al. Northey, Joseph Michael, Nicolas Cherbuin, Kate Louise Pumpa, Disa Jane Smee, and Ben Rattray. "Review: Exercise interventions for cognitive function in adults older than 50: a systematic review with meta-analysis." British Journal of Sports Medicine, 2018. Vol 52:154–160. http://dx.doi.org/10.1136/bjsports-2016-096587.

Physical Activity Guidelines Advisory Committee Report, 2008: To the Secretary of Health and Human Services. Washington, D.C.: U.S. Dept. of Health and Human Services, 2008. http://www.health.gov/PAGuidelines. Details for this note found at https://health.gov/paguidelines/report/g5_musculo.aspx#_Toc199945425.

Ross, Jonathan. "When Pigs Crunch: A Commonsense Approach to Abdominal Training." ACE Certified News, November 2011. https://www.acefitness.org/certifiednewsarticle/1884/when-pigs-crunch-a-commonsense-approach-to/. Accessed July 20, 2018.

Shearer, Elisa and Jeffrey Gottfried. "News Use Across Social Media Platforms 2017." http://www.journalism.org/2017/09/07/news-use-across-social-media-platforms-2017/. Accessed June 8, 2018.

Statistic Brain Research Institute. "Gym Membership Statistics," August 30, 2017. https://www.statisticbrain.com/gym-membership-statistics/. Accessed December 13, 2017.

Strengthwear.us. "Eleiko Lifting Safety Basics." https://www.strengthwear.us/blogs/news/18499963-eleiko-lifting-safety-basics. Accessed January 10, 2018.

Sullivan, Jonathon M. and Andy Baker. The Barbell Prescription. Wichita Falls, TX: The Aasgaard Company, 2016.

USA Weightlifting. "Olympic Lifting College Courses." https://www.teamusa.org/USA-Weightlifting/Coaching/Olympic-Lifting-College-Courses. Accessed December 20, 2017. [Note: USAW links not working at publication time.]

USA Weightlifting. "University Programs." https://www.teamusa.org/USA-Weightlifting/Clubs-LWC/University-Programs. Accessed December 20, 2017.

Watson S.L., B.K. Weeks, et al. "High-Intensity Resistance and Impact Training Improves Bone Mineral Density and Physical Function in Postmenopausal Women With Osteopenia and Osteoporosis: The LIFTMOR Randomized Controlled Trial." Journal of Bone and Mineral Research 33 no. 2 (February 2018): 211-220. doi: 10.1002/jbmr.3284.

———. "Heavy Resistance Training Is Safe and Improves Bone, Function, and Stature in Postmenopausal Women with Low to Very Low Bone Mass: Novel Early Findings From The LIFTMOR Trial." Osteoporosis International 26 no. 12 (December 2015):2889-94. doi: 10.1007/s00198-015-3263-2.

Westcott, Wayne L. "Resistance Training is Medicine: Effects of Strength Training on Health." Current Sports Medicine Reports 11 (July/August 2012), 209–216. doi: 10.1249/JSR.0b013e31825dabb8.

Strong Bodies, Strong Business
was set in 10-point Alegreya type,
a much-praised, twenty-first century typeface
designed by Juan Pablo de Peral of Mendoza, Argentina.
Book designer is Amanda Warren Martin.

www.ingramcontent.com/pod-product-compliance
Lightning Source LLC
Chambersburg PA
CBHW032150020426
42334CB00016B/1259